Jane Austen

Twayne's English Authors Series

Herbert Sussman, Editor
Northeastern University

TEAS 498

Jane Austen

John Lauber

Twayne Publishers ■ New York

Maxwell Macmillan Canada ■ Toronto

Maxwell Macmillan International ■ New York Oxford Singapore Sydney

Jane Austen
John Lauber

Copyright 1993 by Twayne Publishers

Twayne Publishers   Maxwell Macmillan Canada, Inc.
Macmillan Publishing Company 1200 Eglinton Avenue East
866 Third Avenue   Suite 200
New York, New York 10022   Don Mills, Ontario M3C 3N1

Library of Congress Cataloging-in-Publication Data

Lauber, John, 1925-
    Jane Austen / John Lauber.
    p. cm. – (Twayne's English authors series; TEAS 498)
    Includes bibliographical references and index.
    ISBN 0-8057-7014-3
    1. Austen, Jane, 1775-1817 – Criticism and interpretation.
I. Title. II. Series.
PR4037.L38 1993
823'.7 – dc20   93-3788
                                                           CIP

The paper used in this publication meets the minimum requirements of American National Standard for Information Sciences – Permanence of Paper for Printed Library Materials, ANSI Z39.48-1984.

10 9 8 7 6 5 4 3 2 1

Printed in the United States of America.

Contents

Chronology

1775	Jane Austen born at village of Steventon, England, to George and Cassandra Austen.
1785-1787	With her sister, Cassandra, Austen attends the Abbey School in Reading, England.
1790-1793	Writes her juvenilia.
1795-1798	Writes original versions of *Northanger Abbey*, *Sense and Sensibility*, and *Pride and Prejudice*.
1797	"First Impressions" (original version of *Pride and Prejudice*) rejected by a London publisher.
1801	Father retires and moves to Bath with his wife and daughters.
1803	*Susan* (original version of *Northanger Abbey*) is bought by a publisher but never issued.
1804	Austen begins, and quickly abandons, "The Watsons."
1805	Death of father, George.
1808	Moves to Southampton with mother and sister.
1809-1817	Lives with her mother and sister in a small house provided by her wealthy brother Edward in the village of Chawton, in southern England. Begins revising original versions of *Sense and Sensibility* and *Pride and Prejudice*.
1811	*Sense and Sensibility* published.
1813	*Pride and Prejudice* published.
1814	*Mansfield Park* published. Austen begins work on *Emma*.
1816	*Emma* is published and is dedicated to the Prince Regent (future George IV) at his request. Austen completes *Persuasion*.

1817   Composes the fragment "Sanditon"; abandons it be-
            cause of incapacitating illness. Austen is moved to
            Winchester for medical care in May and dies there on
            18 July. Buried in Winchester Cathedral on 24 July.

1818   *Northanger Abbey* and *Persuasion* published jointly in
            a four-volume edition, with a biographical preface of
            Austen by her brother Henry.

Chapter One

Austen: The Life and the Work

Jane Austen was born on 16 December 1775 in the village of Steventon in central England. Like the heroes, and also the fools, of several of her novels, her father, George Austen, was an Anglican clergyman, the rector of Steventon. Jane's mother, Cassandra, was a minister's daughter. It must have been a crowded household, with two daughters and five brothers (besides a sixth, apparently retarded and deaf, who was cared for away from home). The Austens were far from rich, and to supplement his income George Austen prepared boys for university, tutoring them in his home. Still, they lived comfortably enough. There seems to have been money for books (an expensive luxury), and the family kept horses and a carriage, an important mark of status.

By manners and education, as well as by George Austen's profession and the careers chosen by his sons (the navy, the church, banking), the family could legitimately claim to be gentry, while background and income were at least "respectable" – a key word in the social vocabulary of the time and in Austen's novels. (One son, Edward, was adopted by distant, childless relatives – a wealthy landowning family – taking their name and eventually inheriting their estate.) The two brothers in the navy would spend much of their time at sea during the long wars with France, but contact was never broken. That family background no doubt accounts for Austen's enthusiastic and knowledgeable presentation of naval affairs and characters, which is not only essential to the action of *Mansfield Park* and *Persuasion* but brings a sense of the greater world into both novels. Not only do her characterizations go well beyond popular stereotypes of the plain, bluff seaman, but she understood as well the difficulties of promotion, the role of luck, and the reward for success in terms of prizes captured and fortunes made.

In late eighteenth-century England, boys of the Austens' class might hope to go to university, or begin training for their profession, but unless the family was wealthy enough to afford a governess, girls could expect at most a few years away from home at a boarding school to pick up what knowledge they could. Throughout the nineteenth century Austen's range of knowledge would be consistently underestimated by her critics, no doubt because she had never been to university and consequently lacked the first-hand knowledge of Greek and Latin classics that was then considered essential to an educated person. No woman, and comparatively few men, could have been considered educated by that standard.

From 1785 to 1787, Jane and her sister, Cassandra, attended a boarding school for girls, the Abbey School in Reading. When she came home formal education had ended, but learning had not. Women of the upper classes usually received some training in music and art, the amount and quality depending largely on the family's wealth. The young Austen acquired several of the proper female "accomplishments" – she sang, she played the piano reasonably well, she did not paint or draw but was proud of her skill at sewing and embroidery, and she greatly enjoyed dancing. Ballroom scenes would be of crucial importance in her novels, but none of her heroines is notable for "accomplishments." More important, for a future author, her father's substantial library was open to her, apparently without restriction. (Family libraries provided an essential source of education for female writers in the nineteenth century.) The Austens were not only a lively and affectionate family, but an unusually literate one as well.

Reading aloud in the family circle – fiction and nonfiction, poetry and drama – was a favorite amusement of the time, and practiced regularly by the Austens. (Henry Crawford, in *Mansfield Park*, would be notable for his ability to make a Shakespearean text come to life.) If novels pleased, they might then be read individually. Certainly, as a young woman, Austen read widely and eagerly, familiarizing herself with the poetry and periodical essays of the middle and later eighteenth century. Samuel Johnson was a special favorite, particularly his *Rambler* essays, and occasionally an elaborate Johnsonian sentence appears in her own writing. She read widely in the novel, both those of her own time and of the recent past. Samuel Richardson's enormous *Sir Charles Grandison*, presenting a model hero in four volumes, became a lifelong favorite. The Gothic novels of Ann Radcliffe (particularly her *Mysteries of Udolpho*) and her imitators would give Austen material for satire and parody in *Northanger Abbey*, while Fanny Burney's enormously popular *Evelina* and *Cecilia* showed the success that a woman writer could achieve by mingling comedy and romance. She also read plays. Although a clergyman, George Austen had no puritanical prejudice against the theater, and plays might be read aloud or even performed, with productions improvised by the family and friends in the drawing room or in a summer theater in the barn. Recollection of those amateur theatricals would provide Austen with a key episode in *Mansfield Park*. (Fanny Price's disapproval of the Mansfield theatricals does not necessarily signal any change of attitude on Austen's part; it is appropriate both to Fanny's character and to the circumstances.)

In that encouraging atmosphere, it is not surprising that Austen herself began to write. Her first compositions were farcical pieces that parodied the fictional styles of the day for her own amusement and her family's. They are available today in the standard edition of her writings (volume 6, *Minor Works*) edited by R. W. Chapman.[1]

In retrospect, this early writing constitutes a literary apprenticeship. Yet it does not seem likely that a girl in that time and place would have deliberately set out to become a professional writer. Marriage was a woman's goal and fulfillment, it was a woman's career – a doctrine accepted by all of Austen's heroines, even Marianne Dashwood of *Sense and Sensibility*, who defies so many social conventions. And while waiting for marriage, Austen paid visits, she flirted, she danced ("There were twenty dances and I danced them all," she wrote to Cassandra in 1798. "I could just as well dance for a week together."[2]) Like most girls of her day, she expected to marry, and one not entirely reliable recollection describes her as "the prettiest, silliest, most affected husband-hunting butterfly" that the writer had ever known.[3]

Ultimately, marriage did not come to Jane Austen. We can guess that her intelligence, as well as her lack of fortune, might have put off some men, but we know comparatively little of Austen's emotional life. There may have been no intimate secrets to reveal, or they may have been lost by the time James Austen-Leigh came to write a memoir of his aunt's life – the first biography – more than 50 years after her death. But if there had been such secrets, he would not have published them. His *Memoir of Jane Austen* is a model of Victorian discretion. And whatever revelations Austen's correspondence might have contained were lost when Cassandra examined the letters after her sister's death and burned everything she considered too private or personal for public purview. Cassandra herself became engaged, but her fiancé died of fever in the West Indies. She too remained single, and the sisters' relationship would become the closest, most significant of their lives.

As she passed her mid-20s, Austen began to take her writing more seriously. By the late 1790s, she had composed three novels, early versions of *Sense and Sensibility*, *Pride and Prejudice*, and *Northanger Abbey*, reading the works to her family when they were finished. In the fall of 1797 her father wrote to a London publisher, Cadell and Davies, on his daughter's behalf, offering the manuscript of a three-volume novel – probably "First Impressions," the future *Pride and Prejudice*. His offer was rejected by return mail. If Cadell and Davies had been more encouraging, Austen's career as a published writer might have begun 10 or 12 years earlier than it did, and we might have another half-dozen novels at least.

In 1801, George Austen retired with his wife and daughters to Bath, where he died several years later. It was an unhappy time for his younger daughter, who missed her old friends and relations and could not accustom herself to town life. (Bath becomes a background, rather unfavorably presented, in two of Austen's novels – *Northanger Abbey* and *Persuasion*.) Austen was 27 at the time of that move, and an opportunity for marriage seems to have come her way that summer, only to be snatched away. Details are uncertain, but apparently while at a seaside village in Devon, she met a charming, intelligent, and unmarried clergyman. They were instantly and strongly attracted to each other, but soon the man was called away, leaving Austen expecting a proposal by letter. Instead, word came a few weeks later that he had died in a sudden illness.

A few months afterward, while visiting friends in December 1801, Austen accepted a proposal of marriage from Harris Biggs-Wither, an awkward, stammering young man of 21 who was a landowner. Instead of facing a possible future of genteel poverty, she could become the mistress of a great house, in a countryside that she loved. Unfortunately, as she almost immediately recognized, she and young Biggs-Wither were hopelessly incompatible, and the next morning she broke the engagement, surely realizing that she would probably never have another chance to marry. There is no evidence of any future romance or offer of marriage.

Perhaps in consequence of that surely painful and embarrassing event, the age of 27 seems to have acquired a special significance for Austen. The 17-year-old Marianne Dashwood declares, in *Sense and Sensibility*, that a "woman of seven-and-twenty can never hope to feel or inspire affection." In *Pride and Prejudice* Charlotte Lucas, 27 and like Austen facing the specter of spinsterhood, saves herself from that fate by marrying the foolish Mr. Collins, declaring in justification, "I am not romantic, you know." But Austen's final novel, *Persuasion*, directly refutes Marianne's belief that only the very young can truly love. Anne Elliot, at 27, loves more deeply than any other Austen heroine and can inspire passion as well.

George Austen died early in 1805, but his wife and daughters stayed in Bath for two more years, with a drastically diminished income. In 1808 there was a temporary move to Southampton, where they expected to live with Jane's brother Frank, who planned to marry and make his home there. But a better solution soon presented itself. In 1809, Jane Austen's brother Edward, now a great landowner, gave his mother and sisters a cottage in the village of Chawton, 50 miles southwest of London and near his estate of Godmersham. (Restored by the Jane Austen Society, the house is today open to visitors.) There, Austen would live quietly until a few months before her death in 1817, enjoying again the security of a true home, with country walks, village society, household duties, and occasional visits to brother Henry, a London banker, and to Edward and his family at Godmersham. Nephews and nieces began to provide a substitute for the family life at Steventon. Now, in the physical and emotional security of Chawton – conditions that seem to have been essential for her work – Austen began to write seriously again.

In the 10 years before the move to Chawton, she seems to have written only "The Watsons," a fragment of fewer than 20,000 words, apparently abandoned in 1804. One of the novels composed earlier – "Susan" (the original version of *Northanger Abbey*) – had been sold to a publisher, Crosby and Company, in 1803 for £10 and was even included in a list of forthcoming books, but for unknown reasons was never issued. Now, in a peaceful village, with a settled home and way of life, Austen returned to her writing, first revising

"Elinor and Marianne," retitling it *Sense and Sensibility*. ("I am never too busy to think of S & S," she wrote to Cassandra during a visit to London: "I can no more forget it than a mother can forget her sucking child" [*Letters*, 272]). Both *Sense and Sensibility* and *Pride and Prejudice* seem to have been originally written as "epistolary novels" – that is, the story was told through letters written by the characters to each other. In *Sense and Sensibility*, in particular, the revision must have been drastic, since in the novel as we have it, the two principal characters, Elinor and Marianne Dashwood, are never separated and have no occasion for exchanging letters.

A publisher was found, Thomas Egerton of London, with the author paying the cost of publication and earning a royalty if her book sold well (a common arrangement), and in the fall of 1811 *Sense and Sensibility* appeared, but without the author's name. "By a Lady" read the title page. The first edition sold out and a second printing was required, earning £140 for Austen – a substantial amount of money for the time.

No doubt encouraged by the publication of *Sense and Sensibility* and surely delighting in her own renewed creativity, Austen turned next to "First Impressions," revising it and retitling it *Pride and Prejudice*. Published in the winter of 1813, it too was well received. If it could not make readers weep and offered no harrowing adventures, then its wit and its realism offered compensation. There can be deep feeling in Austen's books, but there is little crying – her sales might have been better if she had made her readers weep. As for the author, the book was "her own darling child" and its heroine, Elizabeth Bennet, "as delightful a creature as ever appeared in print" (*Letters*, 297) – a judgment that generations of readers have agreed with. *Pride and Prejudice* brought the author £110 (this time she had sold the copyright instead of receiving royalties) and went through two more editions in the next four or five years. Her lifetime earnings from her writing would come to about £600. This was a significant amount, particularly for a woman, at a time when a skilled workman could support a family on considerably less than a £100 a year, although not to be compared with the fortunes earned by her famous contemporaries, Byron and Scott.

Austen remained anonymous, but the title page of *Pride and Prejudice* had identified her as the author of *Sense and Sensibility*.

With two of the three early novels disposed of, and the third, the future *Northanger Abbey*, put aside, she had a new novel, *Mansfield Park*, well under way before the publication of *Pride and Prejudice*. She would not repeat herself – *Mansfield Park* was a longer and far more serious book than *Pride and Prejudice*, and also less popular, both in Austen's time and later. It has always been a favorite with a few readers, however, and in the twentieth century has probably attracted more critical attention than any other Austen novel. It appeared in May 1814 with the byline, "By the author of *Sense and Sensibility* and *Pride and Prejudice*." *Emma*, her next novel, would be written by "The author of *Pride and Prejudice*" – which is how Austen has been known to the general public ever since.

Emma was issued early in 1816 and dedicated – after a request amounting to a command – to the Prince Regent, the future George IV, who greatly admired Austen's work. (It was an admiration that is not likely to have been reciprocated; the prince was notorious for his licentiousness.) The royal librarian, James Clarke, escorted Austen on a tour of the prince's library in his residence of Carlton House and even proposed that her next novel should be a "historical romance illustrative of the history of the august House of Cobourg" (*Letters,* 451) (a timely topic, as a prince of that family had recently married the daughter of the Prince Regent). Her answer was immediate and direct: "I could no more write a romance than an epic poem" and if required "to keep it up and never relax into laughing. . . I am sure I should be hung before I had finished the first chapter." "No," she concluded, "I must keep to my own style and go on in my way" (*Letters,* 452).

    Emma too was well received, even though Austen had chosen a heroine whom, she predicted, "no one but myself will much like" (*Memoir,* 157). (Certainly readers have never been as taken with Emma Woodhouse as they have with Elizabeth Bennet.) *Emma* received one distinction that probably mattered much more to its author than royal praise – a long and favorable review in the leading journal *Quarterly Review* that recognized Austen as a practitioner of a new kind of novel – new, that is, in its faithfulness to the circumstances of everyday life. Unfortunately, since reviews were then published anonymously, Austen never knew that her work had been given such flattering attention by the most successful and admired writer of the day, Walter Scott.

Meanwhile, Austen had been at work on her next novel, *Persuasion*, completing the first draft in the summer of 1816 and immediately commencing revision. With its mature and sensitive heroine, who has never recovered from a broken romance eight years earlier, *Persuasion* has seemed to many readers to be almost autobiographical. At the same time, Austen seems to have returned to the early "Susan" (originally composed in 1798-99), retitling it *Northanger Abbey* and preparing it for publication; she drew up a burlesque "Plan of a Novel," ridiculing further suggestions by the ineffable Mr. Clarke and others, as well as satirizing the vacuous sentimentality and absurd improbability of the popular fiction of the day. The heroine would have "much tenderness & sentiment, and no Wit" (*Minor Works*, 428), would suffer greatly (and "occasionally be starved to death"), and her aged father would die "after 4 or 5 hours of tender advice & parental admonition to his miserable Child" (*Minor Works*, 430).

For a little longer, Austen would go on in her own way, even broadening that way. The crucial reconciliation between the heroine and her long-estranged lover in *Persuasion* was rewritten, with an emotional depth she had never before achieved, and in January 1817 she commenced a new novel, working on it for the next two months and writing some 24,000 words before putting it aside. Named "Sanditon," after a seaside resort being developed and promoted by two of its principal characters, the work's sharply satirical tone recalls her early writings, but the targets of satire – the visionary or grasping developers and the hypochondriacs who come to Sanditon seeking health – are new. But Austen's strength had been failing for nearly a year, and by the end of March she was too weak to go on writing. She still hoped to live, and in May had herself taken to the nearby cathedral town of Winchester, in search of more effective treatment. But doctors could not help. She died on 18 July 1817, and on 24 July was buried in Winchester Cathedral.

The Chawton years (1809-17) had been productive by any standard, yielding three novels carefully revised and three new novels written, two of these (*Emma* and *Mansfield Park*) long and complex works. All of this was done under conditions that would paralyze many writers. Austen had no room of her own at Chawton, writing instead, as Austen-Leigh tells us in his *Memoir*, in the common sitting room, subject to interruptions from casual visitors, when the manuscript would be whisked out of sight or hidden under a sheet of blotting paper. The hinge of an outer door was never oiled, so that its creaking could warn her of visitors. Her authorship was hardly a secret, but she preferred it to be known to as few people as possible. Such inconveniences surely made composition difficult at times, but Austen's situation had advantages – the security and the support, both economically and psychologically, that she enjoyed – which clearly outweighed its drawbacks.

Still, Austen must have had a remarkable ability to resist distraction to accomplish so much. If *Emma* was completed in only 14 months, she must have been writing several hours a day for most of those days and thinking about her work in progress for much of the remaining time. She was no genteel amateur in those Chawton years, as women were expected to be and as Austen-Leigh's *Memoir* often makes her seem, but a busy and highly productive writer, deeply concerned with the publication and reception of her work – a professional, in the full sense of the term.

Six months after Austen's death, *Persuasion* and *Northanger Abbey* were published in four volumes with a biographical preface by her brother Henry, which made her authorship public for the first time. Henry informed readers that Austen had been "formed for rational and elegant discourse," that she had excelled in dancing, and that "on serious subjects [matters of religion and morality] her opinions accorded strictly with those of our Established Church." Her novels have never been out of print since then.

Chapter Two

Beginnings

The Juvenilia

Austen's "juvenilia" – the pieces she composed between the ages of 12 and 18 – are preserved in three slender manuscript volumes, neatly copied from the originals by the author and entitled, with mock seriousness, "Volume the First," "Volume the Second," and "Volume the Third" (of "The Works of Jane Austen," one supposes), containing principally burlesque narratives that parody the fictional modes of her time and the period just preceding it – particularly as displayed in the cult of sensibility, or sentimentality.

There is, as might be expected, a steadily increasing maturity. "Volume the First" includes a poem ridiculing poetic clichés ("Gently brawling down the turnpike road, / Sweetly noisy falls the Silent Stream," etc.), two playlets – one titled "The Visit," a burlesque of fashionable comedies, and the other appropriately named "The Mystery," in which every speech seems entirely unrelated to those preceding and following it – and 11 brief prose pieces, burlesquing the sentimental fiction of the day. "Volume the Second" carries on the ridicule of sentimental conventions in the 34-page "Love and Freindship" [sic], which for modern readers is easily the most amusing, and intelligible, of all of these sketches. "Volume the Third" is particularly important to Austen scholars, with its long (50 pages) and relatively serious "Catherine, or The Bower," which reads like an abandoned first draft of a novel and clearly foreshadows her future work.

Written to amuse her family and perhaps friends, these pieces were no doubt read aloud in the family circle and would circulate among relatives for many years. Among English novelists, only the Brontë sisters, with their "Gondal" saga, have left as much work from their adolescence. The differences are highly revealing. The Brontës created a fantastic imaginary kingdom, with romantic heroes

11

and heroines who experience intense passions and heroic adventures; Austen's pieces are set in a world bearing at least a recognizable resemblance to the historical England of her day and suggest a
witty, critical intelligence.

In these early writings, Virginia Woolf has remarked, "the girl of
fifteen is laughing at the world."[1] More exactly, the young Austen is
laughing, more or less affectionately, at some of the fictional conventions of her day, principally those of the popular and highly improbable sentimental novels, with their heroes and especially heroines of
incredibly delicate sensibilities. The secret correspondences, the
telling of life histories on the slightest provocation, provided irresistible targets. "Dear Sally," writes a lover in "Amelia Webster," "I
have found a very convenient old hollow oak to put our Letters in,"
then explains (for the reader) "for you know we have long maintained a private Correspondence." "Will you favor us with your Life
and adventures?" one character asks another on first meeting, in
"Jack and Alice," and is immediately favored. There is an abundance
of boisterous farce. In "Frederic and Elfrida: A Novel" (of seven
pages), "the intimacies between the Families . . . daily increased till
. . . they did not scruple to kick each other out of the window on the
slightest provocation." Charlotte, a heroine of great sensibility, accepts the proposals of two suitors on the same day (because she
can't bear to disappoint them), then drowns herself. A young woman
is warned that first loves are dangerous and should be avoided, but
"a second attachment is quite safe." Proprieties are broken in ways
that would never occur in Austen's novels: "the Bottle being pretty
briskly pushed about . . . the whole party . . . were carried home,
Dead Drunk." Exaggerated emotion is endlessly ridiculed. A heroine
disappointed in love, "retiring to her own room, continued in tears
the remainder of her Life." Austen also makes fun of the conventions
of the novel in letters: a heroine writes to inform a friend that she
did not stop at the friend's house last Monday, adds that she "has
many things to inform you of," and immediately breaks off with "my
Paper reminds me of concluding; & beleive me yr ever &c."

The young satirist does not limit herself to fiction. The solemnity,
the clichés, the pretended objectivity of history and historians are
burlesqued in "The History of England from the reign of Henry 4th
to the death of Charles 1st." A brief account of the reign of Henry IV
commences with "Henry the 4th ascended the throne of England

much to his own satisfaction in the year 1399, after having prevailed on his cousin . . . Richard the 2nd, to resign it to him, and to retire for the rest of his life to Pomfret Castle, where he happened to be murdered." As for the closing of the monasteries by Henry VIII, "his abolishing Religious Houses and leaving them to the ruinous depredations of time has been of infinite use to the landscape of England." And in the time of Charles I, only five men in England never "swerved from their attachment to his Majesty," one of them being "the King himself . . . stedfast in his own support."

History is seen as principally an account of scandals and murders, told with blatant partisanship (it is a judgment not very far from Voltaire's opinion that history is a record of the crimes and follies of humanity). Austen will return to the theme in *Northanger Abbey*, when Catherine Morland declares that history is made up of nothing but "the quarrels of popes and kings . . . wars or pestilences on every page; the men all so good for nothing, and hardly any women at all."[2] Written history, as Austen well knew, was a record of the actions of men, written by men. But novelists had already begun to supply that unwritten history of women.

The most developed of these pieces, and the most amusing to the present-day reader, is "Love and Freindship," written when Austen was 15. Thirty-two pages long, it is a detailed burlesque of the epistolary novel, with all its improbabilities, and of the cult of sensibility – an incredible sensitivity, particularly to landscapes, combined with the immediate and full expression of every emotion. "Sensibility" in practice can be intensely egotistical, as "Love & Freindship" demonstrates. As Laura, the heroine, recounts her life history, she modestly admits her own perfection – perfect beauty, combined with mastery of every female accomplishment – and admits only one fault: "A sensibility too tremblingly alive to every affliction of my Freinds, my Acquaintance and particularly to every affliction of my own."

The dialogue continually satirizes fictional clichés – what Austen would later call "novel slang": "My father, seduced by the false glare of Fortune and the Deluding Pomp of Title, insisted on giving my hand to Lady Dorothea." The hero rejects the bride chosen for him by his father, although she is "Lovely and Elegant in her Person . . . Easy and polite in her Address," because she belongs to the "Inferior order of Beings," lacking in "Delicate Feeling, tender Sentiments, and refined Sensibility." (As proof of this deficiency, she is in the company of the heroine for 30 minutes without either confiding any of her secret thoughts or asking the heroine to confide in her.)

Emotional responses are instant and overwhelming. When the heroine encounters a girl who appears sympathetic, "We flew into each other's arms . . . exchanged vows of mutual Freindship for the rest of our lives" and "instantly unfolded to each other the most inward secrets of our Hearts." And at the reunion of the hero and his closest friend, the two girls are so deeply moved that they "fainted alternately on a sofa." They regularly faint, on the sofa or in each others' arms, through the rest of the story.

Both the moral implications and the fictional conventions of the novel of sensibility are satirized. "Sensibility" in practice is revealed as callous egotism. "It is my greatest Boast that I have incurred the displeasure of my Father!" the hero declares, before escaping with the heroine in his father's carriage. Financing their travels with money he "gracefully purloined from his unworthy father's Escritoire," the lovers journey through England and Scotland, making converts to sensibility, leaving unpaid debts, and generally spreading havoc wherever they go. The standard recognition scene is hilariously burlesqued. As Laura, Sophia (her friend), and Augustus (the hero) enter an inn, they experience the ultimate recognition scene when Laura encounters the grandfather she has never seen (but knows at once "through an instinctive Sympathy"). Sophia, her friend, appears, and is recognized as another grandchild. Two doors open in succession and two handsome young men enter, revealing themselves as yet more grandchildren – at which the old gentleman inquires fearfully whether he has any other grandchildren in the house, then hands each one £50 and rushes out.

After being separated from their husbands, the two heroines are left "weltering in their blood" by the highway after an accident to their carriage. "Sophia shreiked [*sic*] and fainted on the ground," writes the narrator. "I screamed and instantly ran Mad." Love must be felt at first sight: on first beholding Edward, the heroine feels "that on him the happiness or Misery of my future Life must depend." It's worth noting that in Austen's mature work, love at first sight occurs only once, in Marianne Dashwood's disastrous passion for Willoughby in *Sense and Sensibility*.

Consciously or not, the 15-year-old Jane Austen was doing, on a smaller scale, what Cervantes had done in *Don Quixote:* disposing of an outworn literary mode through ridicule. The important difference is that in Cervantes's novel the convention of knight-errantry remains noble in spite of its impracticality in the often squalid everyday world, and Don Quixote appears both absurd and admirable, while Laura's "sensibility" is revealed as no more than a mask for selfish egotism. This kind of "Quixotism" – treated more sympathetically – will reappear in *Northanger Abbey*, when Catherine Morland begins to believe that she is living in a Gothic novel, and (this time very nearly bringing tragic consequences), in *Sense and Sensibility*, when Marianne Dashwood tries to practice the impossible ideal of "sensibility" – which may be roughly defined as an extraordinary sensitivity to all impressions and the instant and full expression of all emotions. Like the absurd heroines of "Volume the First" and "Volume the Second," Marianne seems to have acquired sensibility from her reading.

"Volume 3" is less entertaining, but even more revealing. In its two long pieces, "Catherine" (50 pages) and "Lady Susan" (68 pages), the parodist becomes the apprentice novelist. "Catherine" offers the first recognizable Austen heroine – a sensible young woman, quietly witty, who is considerably more intelligent and perceptive than her moralistic and hypochondriac aunt, the fashionable and foolish Camilla, or the ambiguous Edward Stanley, Camilla's handsome and lively brother, who appears and disappears abruptly, without visible reason. Catherine had become strongly attracted to him, and he leaves her in complete uncertainty about his feelings and intentions. And there the story ends, no doubt because the author had either lost interest or had found no reasonable explanation for Stanley's behavior.

A character study of a brilliant, predatory, and totally amoral woman, "Lady Susan," by contrast, seems an unsuccessful experiment in a mode that is unique in Austen's serious work. Its protagonist – "heroine" seems inappropriate – is a fashionable, brilliant, and outwardly charming widow of 35 or thereabouts who is simultaneously carrying on an affair with the rakish Manwaring, who is unfortunately married, and scheming to marry the wealthy and naive young Reginald de Courcy. She is also trying to get rid of a 16-year-old daughter, whom she hates, by marrying her to the wealthy and foolish Sir James Martin, but the daughter has fallen in love with de Courcy.

There is material here for a full-length novel, but Austen has squeezed it into 65 pages. She may have found the subject unsuitable, and she clearly had become impatient with the convention of the novel-in-letters form: "This correspondence, by a meeting between some of the parties & a separation between the others, could not, to the great detriment of the Post office Revenue, be continued longer," she comments, then sums up the remaining events in three pages. (Surprisingly, poetic justice is not inflicted on the scheming, heartless Lady Susan. She finally marries Sir James herself, thus getting, if not her first choice, at least a rich, infatuated, and easily managed husband. (In her character, although not in her final success, Lady Susan at times seems to anticipate Becky Sharpe, of Thackeray's *Vanity Fair*.)

"Lady Susan" was an unsuccessful experiment – perhaps a necessary one. In the next few years Austen would produce early versions of her first two published novels, *Sense and Sensibility* and *Pride and Prejudice*, as well as *Northanger Abbey*, which would be published, without major revision, after her death.

Northanger Abbey

The connection of *Northanger Abbey* with Austen's juvenilia is clear. It is intensely literary, much more so than any of her mature works. Not only is there far more discussion of books and reading by its characters than in any other Austen novel, but from the opening sentence the author constantly reminds us that we are reading a fiction. Catherine is "in training for a heroine," we are told in the first chapter, and the Allens, "probably aware that if adventures will not befall a young lady in her own village, she must seek them abroad," invite her to go with them. The tone of that passage clearly indicates that Catherine's "adventures" are likely to be comic, even farcical, and so they prove to be. (But her emotions are to be taken more seriously.) And as the novel nears its end, all pretenses to "realism" are apparently abandoned as the author remarks that her readers "will see in the tell-tale compression of the pages before them, that we are all hastening together toward perfect felicity," and consequently will not share the anxieties of the heroine and the hero. Paradoxically, in pointing out convention and openly acknowledging its fictionality, *Northanger Abbey* makes an implicit claim to greater realism, or perhaps more accurately to greater truthfulness, than other novels.

Again, as in the juvenilia, Austen burlesques a popular literary form, this time the newly fashionable Gothic novel – principally a single novel, Ann Radcliffe's enormously successful *The Mysteries of Udolpho*, published in 1794. But while *Northanger Abbey* begins as burlesque, not only of the Gothic but often of fictional conventions in general, it transforms itself into a novel – a comic novel, of course. Burlesque continues, notably in the Gothic parody of volume 2,[3] but is related to character, functioning primarily as a part of the heroine's education. To Austen, this means not rejection but recognition of fantasy for what it is and acceptance of the actualities of life in late eighteenth-century England as in fact richer and more satisfying than the worlds of sensational fiction.

Catherine Morland is not only the youngest of Austen's heroines but also the most naive and ignorant, of both books and the world. In the course of the novel, she will commit highly embarrassing (but not fatal) blunders, suffer painful embarrassment frequently, be courted by a suitor whom she comes to dislike intensely, learn to discriminate between book-inspired fantasies and reality, experience the difference between false and true friendship, meet and fall in love with a man who is older and more mature than herself, and eventually marry him in spite of the superior wealth and connections of his family and the opposition of his domineering father.

Like her creator, Catherine is the daughter of an Anglican clergyman and a member of a large family. But none of Austen's novels is autobiographical, and Catherine is far more ignorant and naive than the young Austen could have been, and entirely unliterary, preferring "cricket, base ball, riding on horseback, and running about the country at the age of fourteen, to books." Catherine has no objection to books, however, provided they are "all story and no reflection." As for the fashionable female "accomplishments," she has acquired not a one of them. (None of Austen's heroines will be notable for such accomplishments.) At 15, Catherine is "almost pretty," but even at 17 she has never shown the least interest in any male.

If there is to be a novel, Catherine must enter the world, and if she is to become truly adult, she must suffer. Both of these conventions are satisfied as the heroine falls in love and eventually, after the inevitable barriers are overcome, marries the man she loves. The obstacle in *Northanger Abbey* is simply General Tilney's belief that Catherine's parents are not rich or grand enough to make her acceptable as a wife for his son, but in later novels the barriers may be more complex and more interesting. The heroine, for example, may be blinded by her own prejudice or pride until she is finally able to recognize her own needs and desires and so to satisfy them by marriage to the man of her choice – as is the case with Elizabeth Bennet and Emma Woodhouse. And there the story will end. But while the basic pattern appears clear and simple, it is distinctively varied in each of the novels.

Catherine, then, must leave the security of home and enter the world, as represented by the town of Bath, the most popular and fashionable resort in England, where ladies and gentlemen went to cure their ailments by taking the waters and to escape the monotony of country life. Bath is sophisticated; it offers a variety of human types (including of course young men) that a girl from a village rectory could never have encountered at home. In Bath, Catherine will learn to discriminate between true and false friendship and to trust her own responses. And as readers surely expect, there she will begin to fall in love – a process presented as entirely natural and predictable when an unsophisticated girl meets a witty and charming young man who pays attention to her.

Bath offers not only social variety but a freedom that Catherine has never experienced before. Nominally, she is under the protection of neighbors, Mr. and Mrs. Allen, but in fact she is generally left to her own devices. Such nearly total freedom no doubt was highly uncommon for young women then, but whatever the historical realities of the time may have been, Austen's heroines are always active in shaping their own destinies. Mrs. Allen, who ought to supervise her young charge, is principally interested in observing the current fashions or in pricing muslins in the shops. She is what might be called a negative fool, in contrast, for example, to Mrs. Bennet in *Pride and Prejudice;* Mrs. Allen is no doubt equally foolish, in her own fashion, but she is hardly more than a vacancy, while Mrs. Bennet is undeniably a presence.

Guardians, whether parents or not, are always inadequate in Austen's novels. They are careless and indifferent (like Mr. Bennet in *Pride and Prejudice* or Sir Walter Elliot in *Persuasion*), or foolish (like Mrs. Bennet), or helpless (like Mr. Woodhouse in *Emma*), or blinded to reality (as is Sir Thomas Bertram to the true character of the Crawfords in *Mansfield Park* or Mrs. Dashwood to the dangers in Willoughby's courtship of Marianne in *Sense and Sensibility*). This inadequacy does not necessarily reflect actual social conditions – there seems no reason to suppose that parents were particularly irresponsible during Austen's lifetime – but it is a fictional necessity, throwing the heroines on their own resources and thus allowing the story to develop. The heroines can be mistaken, but nevertheless they must depend on the accuracy of their judgments and their own responses, which finally guide them correctly.

Experiencing the new and unpleasant emotion of loneliness in a crowd, Catherine eagerly accepts the friendship of the fashionable and man-hunting Isabella Thorpe, who is engaged to Catherine's oldest brother, James (but Isabella, we soon realize, does not take either engagements or friendship seriously), and accepts at least the company of Isabella's brother John. An essential part of Catherine's education will be to recognize and admit the falsity of Isabella's friendship and to acknowledge that John Thorpe, James's intimate friend, with his oaths, his bluster, his incessant boasting about his own abilities and about everything that belongs to him, is a fool, a bore, and a braggart, in short, a crude stereotype of masculinity.

Technically, Thorpe represents a character type that will appear in each of Austen's novels and that she names the "anti-hero" (*Minor Works*, 430). Austen's antihero is the more or less disreputable male who offers himself as a rival to the hero for the heroine's love. That Catherine has gained maturity is apparent in her easy evasion of Thorpe's clumsy efforts at a proposal:

> "Did you ever hear the old song, 'Going to one wedding brings on another?'
> [referring to the expected marriage of his sister to Catherine's brother.] I say,
> will you come to Belle's wedding, I hope?"
>   "Yes; I have promised your sister to be with her, if possible."
>   "And then you know" – twisting himself about and forcing a foolish
> laugh – "I say, then you know, we may try the truth of this same old song."
>   "May we? – but I never sing."

John Thorpe has offered a test of Catherine's power of perception that she easily passes.

The case of Isabella is more difficult. To the naive Catherine, her new friend is glamorous and sophisticated, while her friendship, of course, seems genuine. With Isabella's desertion of James Morland, Catherine is forced to admit that her friend has been false. It's more difficult for her to recognize that for all of Isabella's lavish professions, her "friendship" was as empty as her "love," in spite of her assurances that "my attachments are always excessively strong."

But Isabella has another role besides that of false friend, a role at least equally important – she introduces Catherine to the Gothic novel and the delights of literary terror. Under her tutelage, Catherine reads *Udolpho*, shuddering over the mystery of what lies behind the "dreadful black veil" in the villainous Montoni's castle, high in the Italian Alps. Isabella even provides a reading list: "Castle of Wolfenbach, Clermont, Mysterious Warnings, Necromancer of the Black Forest, Midnight Bell, Orphan of the Rhine, and Horrid Mysteries." Those titles alone, all genuine, almost define the Gothic genre.

The test of a Gothic novel is the degree of fear and horror that it arouses – "Are they all horrid, are you sure they are all horrid?" inquires Catherine. She is assured that they are. Yet the form is not condemned outright in *Northanger Abbey*; the ridicule is almost affectionate. As Henry Tilney, a man of intelligence and taste, observes when Catherine remarks that gentlemen must read better books than novels, "The person who has no pleasure in a good novel, must be intolerably stupid," adding that after beginning *Udolpho*, he could not lay it down for two days – "my hair standing on end the whole time." Catherine's fascination, then, is not to her discredit – it is only her naive belief that evil requires Gothic trappings that must be disproved.

If there is to be a novel at all, by the convention that Austen accepts, the heroine must encounter a hero – defined simply as the man she marries or is about to marry when the novel ends. And so in chapter 3 Catherine encounters the witty and sophisticated Tilney (whose conversation offers a striking contrast to Thorpe's incoherent bluster) and is attracted to him at once – thus matching the most intellectual of Austen's heroes with the most ignorant of her heroines. One critic, Allison Sulloway, sees Tilney as guilty of crushing Catherine's individuality with his irony – "Catherine Morland first learns to feel anxious and ashamed of herself in the presence of the mocking Henry Tilney"[4] – but the text offers no evidence for such a destructive effect. Austen appears to believe, on the contrary, that to point out error is one of the most valuable services that one human being can perform for another. And while it's true that Henry's irony plays on many topics, including at times Catherine's ignorance and naiveté, she surely needs instruction, and instruction cannot help revealing ignorance. In any case, teaching does not necessarily destroy the pupil's self-confidence and individuality. As *Northanger Abbey* demonstrates, the influence of Henry and his sister, Eleanor, on Catherine is beneficial. She finds not only a lover and eventually a husband in him, but a true friend in his sister – in sharp contrast to the pretended friendship of Isabella.

In this novel, the Gothic mode represents the world of fantasy, and temporary excursions there may be harmless and enjoyable. But "reality" is richer by far, even when prosaic. Nothing could be more probable, or less romantic, than Catherine's meeting with Henry Tilney. Both are newcomers in Bath, both are without partners at one of the regular dances, and they are introduced to each other by the master of ceremonies. Tilney is "four or five and twenty" (and therefore far more experienced than Catherine – Austen's heroes are always older than her heroines), has "a pleasing countenance, a very intelligent and lively eye," and "if not quite handsome, was very near it." He is also witty, ironic, and satirical – puzzling qualities for Catherine, which will not be found in any of her other heroes. By the end of chapter 3, then, it seems more than likely that Tilney is to be the hero. His quick intelligence is set off by both the naiveté of Catherine and the confident stupidity of John Thorpe.

In this intensely "literary" novel, so self-conscious of its own fictionality, characters can be confidently placed on the basis of their taste in books. Thorpe promptly disqualifies himself as an eligible suitor, or even companion, with his brusque reply when Catherine, making conversation, asks him if he has ever read *Udolpho:* "Oh, Lord! not I! I never read novels; I have something else to do." (The only novel of the day that he seems to know is Matthew Lewis's *The Monk*, notorious for its eroticism and sadism. He is also familiar with Fielding's *Tom Jones*, which by Austen's time had become morally suspect for the sexual freedom of its hero.)

Breaking through the fictional illusion, Austen has already offered a stirring defense of the novel, for all its frequent absurdities:
"Let us [novelists] not desert one another," she exclaims. "We are an
injured body . . . . there seems almost a general wish of decrying the
capacity and undervaluing the labour of the novelist, and of slighting
the performances which have only genius, wit and taste to recommend them." She imagines a reader laying down her book when
asked what she is reading and answering apologetically, "Only a
novel." By this snobbish, affected contempt, such a reader deprives
herself of both pleasure and knowledge: "only some work in which
the greatest powers of the mind are displayed," the narrator exclaims, "in which the most thorough knowledge of human nature,
the happiest delineation of its varieties, the liveliest effusions of wit
and humour are conveyed to the world in the best chosen language." (And as Austen certainly knew, male chauvinism played its
part in this depreciation of the only literary genre in which many of
the writers and the majority of readers were female.) A discriminating
taste in novels serves as a touchstone of character and intelligence in
Northanger Abbey.

If Henry Tilney can be witty and satirical, Austen is wittier still, as
well as ironically perceptive concerning male attitudes, observing
that while some men consider absolute "imbecility" as a necessary
part of a woman's charm, others (like Tilney) are "too reasonable
and too well informed themselves to desire more in women than ignorance" – a quality that Catherine has in abundance. "A woman,
especially, if she have the misfortune of knowing any thing, should
conceal it as well as she can," observes the narrator. (The bitterness
of that observation is unique in Austen's novels, even when softened
by the implication that ignorance has its social value in men as well,
although to a lesser degree.) And so Tilney lectures on the beauties
of landscape and the nature of the picturesque while Catherine eagerly listens, never suspecting that her ignorance flatters Tilney, and
neither of them realizing that they are falling in love.

The love story is actually completed in volume 1. By its conclusion,
Catherine and Henry have already become attached to each other.
Volume 2 offers a test to Catherine, a puzzle to solve – not the test
or puzzle that she herself finds, or imagines she finds, at Northanger,

but closely related to it. At breakfast with the Tilneys before their departure for Northanger Abbey, she senses a restraint and discomfort in Henry and Eleanor. On the journey itself, she is naively surprised to see that "General Tilney, though so charming a man, seemed always a check upon his children's spirits" and that conversation dies in his presence. Riding in the family coach, to her surprise not even "the incessant attentions of the General himself" can put her at ease. Pleasure returns only when she is freed from his company during the last half of the journey, as she rides with Henry in his curricle (a light, open two-passenger carriage). A question, then, is posed throughout volume 2: What is the true character of General Tilney?

In the scenes at Northanger Abbey, Catherine will come to understand the reality of the General's character, after a wild misinterpretation (when she considers him to be the actual murderer of his wife), which yet is a good deal less far-fetched than it seems. The groundwork is laid for Catherine's imaginings first by the overpowering effect of *Udolpho*, then by Henry's parody of Gothic conventions, as he imagines what she will discover in her room at Northanger: "a ponderous chest which no efforts can open" and a tapestry hiding a padlocked door – which she will nevertheless open, discovering "a dagger, a few drops of blood . . . the remains of some instrument of torture," etc. It is a list of the stock properties of Gothic fiction, which in the event closely parallels what Catherine actually finds. Only scholars are likely to read *Udolpho* today, but the modern reader of *Northanger Abbey* no more needs to be familiar with the Gothic novels of the 1790s than present-day readers of *Don Quixote* need to have read the romances of chivalry that drove Quixote mad. A successful parody recreates its original, and, in any case, the principal "background" needed to appreciate *Northanger Abbey* is simply the recollection of having been young, naive, and inexperienced.

Catherine's mistakes are farcical, of course, but not quite so absurd as she comes to believe – she has, after all, been prepared by her reading and by Henry's warnings. Events follow a predictably recurring pattern, in which Catherine discovers some typically Gothic property – an "immense, heavy chest," "a high, oldfashioned black cabinet" – which she has somehow overlooked and is now determined to open. The opening is predictably delayed (by Catherine's own blunders, as we later learn, when she accidentally locks previously unlocked cabinets or drawers), increasing her fears and the reader's anticipation. Even then at the last moment discovery is dramatically delayed in true Gothic style – "her candle suddenly expires," and the Gothic clichés multiply: "Darkness impenetrable and immoveable filled the room. A violent gust of wind . . . added fresh horror," while from the corridor, "a sound like receding footsteps and the closing of a distant door struck on her affrighted ear." The actual discovery is, again predictably, anticlimactic. The mysterious paper is a laundry list, the innermost drawer contains a neatly folded bedcover. The novels of Radcliffe and her imitators may be known only to an occasional scholar today, but even after 200 years such passages can still amuse, and even, on first reading, create suspense – Austen's parody so powerfully creates the mode it ridicules. (Ridicules but does not destroy – the Gothic seems indestructible.)

In a sense, the conclusion of *Northanger Abbey* the balance between Catherine and Henry Tilney, which has seemed so heavily weighted on his side. With all her blunders, she perceives a deeper reality than the intellectual Henry does. In an obvious sense, his reassurance is correct: Gothic villainy is impossible in a country "where every man is surrounded by a neighbourhood of voluntary spies, and where roads and newspapers lay every thing open." But Catherine's perception is more accurate than his own, as she comes to realize "that in suspecting General Tilney of either murdering or shutting up his wife, she had scarcely sinned against his character, or magnified his cruelty."

The comedy of the final chapters, after Catherine's return home, lies in the contrast between her own reading of her experiences – that they have transformed her, have made her a woman rather than a girl – and her parents' blindness to any change in her. A happy ending, uniting Catherine and Henry, is clearly inevitable – comedies must end with marriage, and in this case probabilities matter very little. As the narrator observes, openly violating the realistic illusion in a way that Austen would never practice in her later novels, readers cannot be expected to share the heroine's anxieties: "the tell-tale compression" of the remaining pages signifies "that we are all hastening together to perfect felicity." Appropriately enough, in a novel as self-consciously fictional as this one, the force of literary convention overpowers considerations of probability and consistency of characterization – although a pretext is given for the General's final approval of Henry's marriage to Catherine. And since in Austen's comedy there are no true "villains" and even the anti-heroes do not really suffer for their faults (unless to go on being what they are can be considered punishment), the General suffers nothing worse than having to change his mind and permit the marriage, and is even allowed to speculate "greedily" on the possibilities of Catherine's inheriting an estate from the wealthy, childless Allens.

Chapter Three

Sense and Sensibility

The title of a French translation of *Sense and Sensibility*, published in 1815 as *Raison et Sensibilité, ou les deux manieres d'aimer* (Reason and Sensibility, or the Two Ways of Loving), neatly sums up the novel's theme. The two ways of loving – that is the primary subject of this novel, although the contrast is wider than that. To compare these "two ways of loving," Austen provides closely paralleling experiences for her heroines. Both Elinor and Marianne fall in love, then appear to have been betrayed by their lovers, and the novel vividly dramatizes their widely differing responses, with the primary heroine (Elinor) guided by sense and the desire to control her grief, while Marianne cultivates and intensifies her suffering, regardless of the consequences to herself and to her family. What happens to each sister matters less than how each deals with her disappointment.

But Austen's title can seem puzzling to the modern reader. *Sense* may be clear enough, but what exactly is *sensibility?* By the end of the novel, that uncertainty is gone – *sensibility* is the set of qualities conspicuously displayed by Marianne Dashwood and pretended to by Marianne's apparent suitor, Willoughby. The term defines itself as Marianne's attitudes and behavior are dramatized – primarily in her rapturous devotion to Willoughby and then in her despair at his treachery, but also in her taste in books and in landscapes, her passion for music, and her contempt for commonplace people and the obligations of everyday social intercourse.

Moral and intellectual qualities can be defined negatively as well as positively. What sensibility is not becomes clear in the second chapter. Mrs. Dashwood and her three daughters – Elinor, Marianne, and Margaret – have lost their husband and father from a sudden illness, leaving them with a modest inheritance of £10,000. By an earlier marriage Mr. Dashwood had a son, John, who has become a highly "respectable" man – that is, he has grown rich through marriage and inheritance. The narrator has already signalled that not much is to be expected from this couple: "He was not an ill-disposed young man, unless to be rather cold-hearted, and rather selfish, is to be ill-disposed,"[1] and his wife "was a strong caricature of himself; – more narrow-minded and selfish." Yet Dashwood begins quite generously, deciding to make a present of £1,000 to each of his half-sisters. His wife objects: "Why was he to ruin himself, and their poor little Harry, by giving away all his money to his half sisters?" She offers practical arguments: "When the money is parted with, it can never return. Your sisters will marry, and it will be gone for ever."

The intended gift is promptly reduced to £500 per sister, then to an annuity of £100 a year for the mother – more useful, John Dashwood reasons, than a gift of cash, which might be quickly spent. But annuities have their risks. As his wife observes, "if Mrs. Dashwood should live fifteen years, we shall be completely taken in . . . people always live forever when there is any annuity to be paid." Husband and wife agree that to be "tied down" to such a payment "takes away one's independence" and that at times it may be very "inconvenient."

The annuity, then is abandoned also; an occasional gift, "a present of fifty pounds, now and then," will serve, and, thinks John Dashwood, "will . . . be amply discharging my promise to my father." Or merely helping his half-sisters and their mother to find a house, or "to move their things," or offering occasional "presents of fish and game" will "strictly fulfill" any promises given, and will be more than enough, considering that Mrs. Dashwood still possesses some handsome china, really too handsome for a woman with her income.

So this eminently respectable couple, as they consider themselves, reason away their obligation to nothing at all, while convincing each other that they are behaving rationally and honorably. What they have displayed is a caricature of *sense*. Yet they do not seem monstrous figures, selfishness embodied. What is frightening about them is precisely their ordinariness and the momentary plausibility of their arguments.

If the quality of *sense* includes a rational regard for the welfare of others, and a sense of one's own obligations, then Mrs. Ferrars, whose son Edward is the nominal "hero," the man whom Elinor loves, can no more represent it than the Dashwoods do. She is more broadly caricatured, a monstrous embodiment of parental tyranny, a true grotesque, both morally and physically. A woman of few words, "proportioning her speech to the number of her ideas," her face is "naturally without expression" but saved from "insipidity" by "a lucky contraction of the brow . . . giving it the strong characters of pride and ill-nature." On discovering that her oldest son, Edward, has foolishly engaged himself to Lucy Steele, a fortune hunter, she is capable not only of disinheriting him but of declaring that if he should enter any profession in order to support himself, she would do everything in her power to prevent him from succeeding. (Behavior, John Dashwood observes, "such as every conscientious good mother . . . would adopt.")

Not every character can be fitted into the dichotomy of *sense-sensibility*. More than any other Austen novel, *Sense and Sensibility* abounds in fools who possess neither quality. Mrs. Ferrars's foppish younger son, Robert, whom we first see through Elinor's eyes while he is shopping for a toothpick case at a Bond Street jeweler's and demanding that every case in the store should be brought out for his inspection, is simply a vain fool – he possesses, as Elinor notes, features of "strong, natural, sterling insignificance." The novel offers other varieties of stupidity in Anne Steele, the vulgar fool, and Sir John Middleton, the sociable fool who cannot exist without company and noise, as well as Lady Middleton, who might be called the insipid fool, interested only in her child, continually exhibiting a reserve with which, the narrator tells us, sense has nothing to do, and Mrs. Palmer, who is merely silly. Nowhere else in Austen's novels is her presentation of social reality more harshly satirical. Society, in *Sense and Sensibility*, seems to offer not much more than a choice between "insipidity" or "insignificance" and malicious stupidity.

As for *sense*, Colonel Brandon, Marianne's eventual husband, cannot represent that quality – he is too shadowy a figure to exemplify anything. Neither can Edward Ferrars, tongue-tied by embarrassment throughout the novel. Certainly Willoughby, Marianne's betrayer, cannot – he guarantees his own unhappiness when he deserts her for a wealthy, bad-tempered heiress. And *sense* cannot be the crass materialism of John Dashwood, advising Elinor on how to catch a wealthy husband: "A very little trouble on your part secures him . . . Some of those little attentions and encouragements which ladies so easily give will fix him in spite of himself."

True sense, then, is precious and correspondingly is rare – displayed only, in this novel, by Elinor Dashwood. What is this *sense?* Common sense, of course – a realistic assessment of people and situations and the possible consequences of one's behavior (all of which the romantic Marianne conspicuously lacks). But it is not simply prudential. As exhibited by Elinor, it appears to be a rational regard for others, a recognition that the world does not exist only to satisfy one's ego (an infantile belief that Marianne sometimes appears to hold), and consequently an acceptance of obligations to others – at which Marianne often fails.

An important ingredient of sense is *candour* – a quality that, as Austen repeatedly reminds us, is lacking in both Marianne and Willoughby. The term can be misleading for present-day readers. For Austen *candour* does not mean frankly admitting one's own failings, or even those of other people, but rather extending charity to others by putting the best possible interpretation on their words and actions. (Jane Bennet, the secondary heroine of *Pride and Prejudice*, is notable for this quality, which her sister Elizabeth quite lacks.) In *Sense and Sensibility*, this virtue is regularly displayed by Elinor, while Marianne and Willoughby consistently fail in it. When Willoughby's desertion of Marianne can no longer be concealed, Colonel Brandon, moved by his anxiety for her, pays a call. Marianne's response, that "A man who has nothing to do with his own time has no conscience in his intrusion on that of others," is a careless, cruel misinterpretation, clearly displaying her lack of "candour."

As for *sensibility*, it is not necessarily the opposite of *sense* or incompatible with it, although an extremist like Marianne seems to believe that it must be. The person of sensibility feels deeply, and fully expresses her feelings, whether of love or anger (regardless of social proprieties, in Marianne's case). *Sensibility* implies also keen sensitivity to landscape and to the arts (to music and poetry, for Marianne). In her juvenilia, Austen had burlesqued the cult of sensibility, presenting it as a mask for egotism and selfishness. But Marianne's sincerity is unquestioned. She stakes her happiness on her principles and nearly loses her life for them. She does, however, resemble Austen's earlier "heroines" in one respect – the inconvenience, and worse, that her behavior brings on others, particularly her sister, and her disregard for the consequences of her behavior.

Marianne is young, intolerant, an absolutist of sensibility. "I could not be happy with a man whose taste did not in every point coincide with my own," she observes at the outset of the novel, and imagines that she has found such a man in Willoughby. Emotion must be intense, or it is unreal. There can be no doubt of the reality of Marianne's grief when she finally acknowledges Willoughby's treachery – it nearly kills her. Yet she is behaving as she believes a woman betrayed in love ought to behave, and her illness is in a sense self-created ("She was without any power, because she was without any desire of command over herself"), but her suffering is genuine. Marianne's agony, as well as the concern of her mother and sister, is so powerfully created that on rereading one is surprised to find that all of this suffering fills only one chapter. Yet her sensibility is not simply to be condemned, dangerous as it can be. Lack of it can produce the cool and rational selfishness of the John Dashwoods.

Sense and Sensibility is not the only Austen novel to present two sharply contrasting heroines. *Pride and Prejudice* does the same with Elizabeth and Jane Bennet; *Emma*, with Emma Woodhouse and Jane Fairfax. In both novels, one heroine – Elizabeth, Emma – is clearly intended to draw most of the reader's interest and concern. It's reasonable to suppose that Austen's intention was similar in *Sense and Sensibility*. Elinor deserves the reader's sympathy by the courage and self-control, as well as the continuing concern for others, that she displays after her own chance of happiness is apparently lost with the revelation of Edward's engagement to Lucy Steele. She is exemplary. As *Sense and Sensibility* concludes, Marianne has apparently become more like her sister, able to recognize the dangers of sensibility and presumably to control its excesses.

The best evidence of Elinor's position as primary heroine is that the novel is told almost entirely from her point of view – Marianne's story is simply included within Elinor's. It's a structure that builds curiosity and suspense, on a first reading, by the mystery that it creates concerning Marianne's relationship to Willoughby. Are they or are they not engaged? All of their behavior suggests that they are, and yet there is no confirmation, no formal interview between the suitor and the mother, and given Marianne's openness, a secret engagement would seem not only improper but impossible. And a careful reader soon has doubts about Willoughby, arising from the apparently unnecessary mystery in which he wraps himself.

Equally suspicious is the fact that at times he almost seems to be Marianne's creation. He "acquiesced in all her decisions, caught all her enthusiasms," we are told. He fulfills her dream of an ideal lover too perfectly. And when the scene moves to London, at midpoint, it soon becomes clear that everything is over between Willoughby and Marianne, although why he behaves with such apparently gratuitous cruelty is explained only when the novel is nearly finished. But above all, the story is consistently presented from Elinor's point of view – never from Marianne's. We are continually shown Elinor's inner responses, her fears and concerns, but Marianne's unspoken feelings are never directly reported – although they are revealed clearly enough!

The form of the novel as well, the standard three-volume pattern (to which four of Austen's six novels conform), indicates Elinor's primacy. At the end of volume 1, she is "mortified," shocked, confounded" by Lucy Steele's revelation of her engagement to Edward. And at the conclusion of volume 2, Elinor's prospects are at their darkest when Lucy is taken into the Harley Street home of the John Dashwoods, seemingly about to be accepted by the family as Edward's future wife. Austen's intentions, then, seem clear, but authorial intentions are not always realized. Energy is an enormously attractive quality, and a character exhibiting it inevitably draws the reader's attention and often sympathy as well.

Marianne can be absurd, as when she solemnly observes that "At my time of life [she is 17] opinions are tolerably fixed. It is not likely that I should now see or hear anything to change them." Her intolerance, her refusal to accept any social obligations, are powerfully communicated, and the moral and aesthetic patterns of the novel clearly require that readers condemn her behavior as irrational, self-destructive, harmful to others. But the difficulty is to do so without condemning *her*. Inevitably, readers sympathize with Marianne because she is truly wronged and because she suffers intensely – more so than any other Austen heroine – and her suffering is powerfully dramatized as her uncertainty about Willoughby's intentions deepens into acute anxiety and, finally, despair, when his treachery is fully revealed.

To some extent, it is true, Marianne is acting a role – behaving as she believes a disappointed heroine ought to. After Willoughby's sudden departure, she "would have thought herself very inexcusable had she been able to sleep at all the first night" after their parting. Grief is cultivated – she "read nothing but what they had been used to read together," she "spent whole hours at the pianoforte, alternately singing and crying," playing over their favorite songs, staring at music that Willoughby had copied for her. Undeniably, she not only intensifies her own misery but makes sure that her mother and sister are miserable as well.

Such an extreme of sensibility – a cultivation of emotion for its own sake, uncontrolled by reason or any sense of concern for others – must lead to disaster. This, Austen's novel powerfully demonstrates. What's more, empathy is entirely lacking in Marianne; she displays no concern for, no sensitivity to the feelings of others. Yet readers are more likely to pity Marianne than to blame her. Her suffering is out of all proportion to her fault, which was simply that of trusting and risking too much, without the security of a formal engagement. Austen's presentation of Marianne is so powerful that her sufferings (even if partly self-imposed) inevitably become more interesting than Elinor's display of self-control. The consequence is that Marianne, even though her behavior is less admirable than Elinor's and her consciousness is never directly presented, often becomes the primary object of concern.

The characterization of Willoughby, particularly during his courtship of Marianne, likewise succeeds. (Given the powerful impression that Willoughby creates, it's surprising to recall in how few pages he actually appears.) At his entry – handsome in his hunting clothes, with dog and gun, carrying the injured Marianne in his arms ("Marianne's preserver," as Margaret, the youngest Dashwood sister, romantically calls him) – he sweeps away caution, except in Elinor. There is a reference to his "manly beauty" – the strongest terms Austen ever uses to describe a man's appearance. His leaving is almost as dramatic as his arrival – "He then departed, to make himself still more interesting, in the midst of a heavy rain." Undeniably, Willoughby displays energy – the only male character in the novel to do so. But doubts soon arise. Is his sensibility genuine, or is he, consciously or not, aping Marianne's? Yet his attraction is undeniable,

making his abrupt and unexplained departure, as well as his brutal
treatment of Marianne in London, all the more mysterious.

Willoughby is the most complex of Austen's antiheroes –
Wickham in *Pride and Prejudice*, Henry Crawford in *Mansfield
Park*, Frank Churchill in *Emma*, Mr. Elliott in *Persuasion*, even the
boorish John Thorpe in *Northanger Abbey*. Ladies are not abducted
in Austen's novels, of course (although the foolish Sir Edward
Denham, in the late fragment "Sanditon," dreams of carrying Clara
Brereton to Timbuctoo, there to work his will upon her). The
antihero is always morally suspect to some degree, but only Wickham, with his seduction of Lydia Bennet, comes close to being a
conventional villain – and that "seduction" obviously occurs with
Lydia's enthusiastic consent. After reading Willoughby's "impudently
cruel" letter to Marianne, Elinor decides that he is "deep in hard-
ened villainy." It is a phrase that the later Austen would have condemned as a cliché – "thorough novel slang" – but that judgment
will be substantially modified.

The role of the antihero in Austen's novels is to provide plot
complications and cause delay, to tempt the heroine (the secondary
heroine, in this case), and to offer a sharp contrast, both psychologically and morally, to the "hero," the man whom the heroine is to
marry at the close of the novel. Certainly Willoughby provides such a
contrast, to Edward Ferrars as well as to Colonel Brandon, who will
become Marianne's husband – although in no other Austen novel
does the antihero overshadow the official hero or heroes as
Willoughby does simply by being so much more interesting. Colonel
Brandon may once have been a man of action, a soldier, but only his
title reminds us of this, and he remains a nonentity throughout.
Willoughby's treachery, his desertion of Marianne, is undeniable, yet
he is finally allowed, near the end of the novel, to confess his guilt
and explain his behavior to Elinor. That unexpected reintroduction
of Willoughby, as impetuous in self-condemnation as he had been in
his lovemaking, together with Elinor's still less expected softening
toward him, helps to save the novel from melodrama by motivating
his behavior and, in retrospect, makes Marianne's passion more
credible.

This meeting between heroine and antihero could easily have
seemed a melodramatic failure, but in fact becomes one of the most
powerful, if not the most powerful, scene in the novel. There is a

sense of liberation, as for once the barriers of propriety, convention, decorum, reserve are swept away – more completely than Marianne ever manages to do. At the most elementary level of interest, the reader's curiosity is satisfied, as Willoughby's behavior is finally explained and his motives revealed. Deeply in debt, he felt that he could not afford to marry for love. Retribution has duly followed, as we learn that after all, Willoughby's betrayal of Marianne hasn't paid – he may have gained money but has trapped himself for life in an unhappy marriage. And Marianne had not simply deluded herself – his love for her had been real.

A necessary explanation, then, is supplied. But the scene accomplishes much more. There is a passion in Willoughby (here a passionate self-condemnation) found nowhere else among the men of Austen's novels. He becomes again, as he had seemed to be in the early chapters, a complex and interesting figure. And he pays a high price for his affair with Eliza, Colonel Brandon's ward – disinheritance, when the wealthy cousin on whom he depended learns of it, with the resulting necessity (as he sees it) of finding a rich wife, and the consequent loss of Marianne. And the complex narrative of his weaknesses, follies, and misdeeds is enlivened by the expressiveness of his language and the force of his self-condemnation: "My business was to declare myself a scoundrel [in the brutal letter he had written to Marianne in London], and whether I did it with a bow or a bluster was of little importance."

Even the restrained Elinor is nearly softened into forgiveness, deciding that "villain" is far too simple a term to apply. ("The world had made him extravagant and vain – Extravagance and vanity had made him cold-hearted and selfish.") In parting, she even takes his hand as a sign of forgiveness. As for Willoughby, to use his own words, he is left to "rub through the world" as best he can, essentially unchanged. His departure is thoroughly characteristic: "God bless you," he exclaims to Elinor, "and with these words, he almost ran out the door."

That is not quite the final word. In relating that interview to Marianne, Elinor, with her usual realism, describes the "certain troubles and disappointments" of comparative poverty and the harassment of debt that would be experienced by a woman married to a man with expensive tastes and little money, for whom "self-denial is a word hardly understood." Her summing up seems unanswerable: "The whole of his behaviour . . . from the beginning to the end of the affair, has been grounded in selfishness." And yet the powerful charm of Willoughby is still felt, poetic justice is not quite inflicted. He has the rich wife that his expensive tastes required, and, we are told, "He lived to exert, and frequently to enjoy himself. His wife was not always out of humour, nor his home always uncomfortable," and he has his dogs and his horses and his hunting to enjoy. And Marianne "remained his secret standard of perfection in woman."

The major weakness of *Sense and Sensibility* lies in its two "heroes," Edward Ferrars and Colonel Brandon, Marianne's eventual husband. Brandon in fact is hardly characterized at all. He is reported to be a man of sense, presumably meaning, among other things, that he is practical and realistic, but he says little and does nothing to support that description, and it is surely contradicted by his action in fighting a duel offstage with Willoughby (in which neither of them is hurt). Willoughby's sneer that Brandon is one of those people "whom every body is delighted to see, and no body remembers to talk to" may illustrate his own lack of "candour," yet seems accurate. Consequently, Marianne's final acceptance of him appears so entirely out of character that the Marianne of the final chapter, destined to become a devoted wife to Brandon and "patroness of a village," seems a changed and diminished figure.

She and her future husband are not even shown together in these concluding chapters. Readers are given only the prophecies of other characters, and of the narrator, that they will marry. It is not surprising, then, that the narrator's assurance that since Marianne could "never love by halves" she would in time become as devoted to Brandon as she had been to Willoughby seems unconvincing. The future foreseen for Willoughby, by contrast, appears thoroughly in character rather than imposed by the author to meet fictional requirements (a heroine must finally marry) and to impress a moral.

The failure of Edward's characterization is not as complete as that of Colonel Brandon, but damages the effect of *Sense and Sensibility* more seriously. Elinor's inner life is open to the reader, as Marianne's is not, and her love for Edward and her anxiety and distress over his engagement to Lucy Steele trouble her continually. Yet Edward hardly seems worth such concern. He is given a touch of self-deprecating wit when early in the novel he sums up his own life for the Dashwoods, listing the professions he had chosen not to prepare himself for, and concluding, "I was therefore entered at Oxford and have been properly idle ever since."

Except for his youthful mistake in engaging himself to Lucy, , Edward is credited with sense, yet in him, *sense* appears to be principally a negative quality. In fact he is characterized by negatives: he has no taste for poetry, no liking for rocks and mountains, he possesses no "peculiar graces of person or address. He was not handsome . . . his manners required intimacy to make them pleasing." Almost the only emotion he displays is acute embarrassment, usually to the point of inarticulateness. And since he is never allowed to express his feelings, and his state of mind is never described, his situation can arouse no interest.

In an Austen novel, characterization depends principally on dialogue, since we are given interior views only of the heroines. A silent character, then, such as Edward or Colonel Brandon, can hardly *have* a character at all. The force of Willoughby's language, in contrast, is striking, particularly in self-condemnation – "the stupid, rascally folly of my own heart." The same criticism, to a lesser degree, can be made of Austen's presentation of Elinor. "Her feelings were strong," we are told, "but she knew how to govern them." And that is the problem – the governing is too complete. Or, to use Austen's terms, sense controls sensibility too easily and too thoroughly. Elinor contains her emotions so successfully that at times it is nearly impossible to feel sympathy for her – particularly since her apparent loss of Edward does not seem to be a very great calamity.

The conclusion both satisfies and frustrates. Austen's reintroduction of Willoughby, allowing him to speak for himself rather than presenting him as a conventional villain, not only explains his highly puzzling behavior, by providing a long-delayed interior view of his characters and motives, but in a sense justifies Marianne's passion. At least she had not been totally deluded – he had loved her. And the manner in which Edward is finally freed from his engagement to Lucy, which he is too honorable to break, is ironic yet convincing – when his mother learns of the engagement, in her rage she not only immediately disinherits him but gives the inheritance he would have had to his foolish younger brother, Robert.

Since an impoverished Edward has no attraction for Lucy, she proceeds to entrap Robert instead, then breaks her engagement to

Edward. So the detestable Mrs. Ferrars gains a daughter-in-law whom she loathes (until Lucy's flattery can win her favor), and Lucy finds a wealthy husband who will no doubt be easier to manipulate than Edward would have been. Lucy's final success, remarks the narrator, provides an example "of what an earnest, an unceasing attention to self-interest . . . will do in securing every advantage of fortune, with no other sacrifice than that of time and conscience." Lucy's punishment, if any, is merely to get what she has wanted. Austen is a moralist, but not a punitive one.

Finally, it is Marianne who remains in the reader's memory. Selfish and absurd she may often be, yet she is very nearly tragic as well, anticipating such nineteenth-century heroines as George Eliot's Maggie Tulliver in *The Mill on the Floss* and Dorothea Brooke in *Middlemarch* or Catherine Linton in Emily Brontë's *Wuthering Heights*, all of whom longed desperately to escape the limitations their society imposed on them.

But there is more to be said than that in her characterization of Marianne, Austen anticipated later female novelists. Here is an overpowering, intensely physical love. Consider Austen's description of Marianne after her rejection by Willoughby, "only half-dressed . . . . kneeling against one of the window seats" for light and "writing as fast as a continual flow of tears would permit her," or, two pages later, lying on her bed with Willoughby's letters beside her, "almost choked with grief," and then, the narrator tells us, "covering her face with her handkerchief, [she] almost screamed with agony."

Sense and Sensibility portrays a woman first swept away in rapturous passion, then physically and emotionally crushed by disappointment and betrayal, until at last she comes very near to literally dying of disappointed love. There is a strength of passion that never recurs in Austen's later novels – that in the whole range of nineteenth-century English fiction is perhaps matched only by Catherine Linton's disastrous passion for Heathcliff.

Sense and Sensibility has seemed to many readers and critics the least characteristic, and the least attractive, of Austen's novels. Tendentious and punitive in its treatment of Marianne, who seems cruelly punished for her sincerity and her passion, the novel can appear to represent a triumph of mediocrity and restraint over passion and sincerity. But such responses overlook the intensity of Austen's satire, not only on the grotesque tyranny of Mrs. Ferrars but on the cool and "rational" egotism of the John Dashwoods, the utter mediocrity of the Middletons, and the single-minded intensity of Lucy Steele's search for a husband who can give her a position in the world. Clearly, readers who dislike irony and satire will find very little satisfaction in Austen's novels in general, while those are baffled by the combination of irony with passion will probably make nothing of *Sense and Sensibility*.

If Marianne anticipates the heroines of the Brontës and of George Eliot, *Sense and Sensibility* overall looks back to the eighteenth century, with its aristocratic rake (Willoughby) and its assortment of social grotesques who can remind one of the ferocious caricatures of artists like Rowlandson and Gillray at the end of the century. Its language, too, can suggest the past, at times echoing the elaborate parallel structures of Samuel Johnson, one of Austen's favorite authors. While shopping on Bond Street, "Mrs. Palmer, whose eye was caught by everything pretty, expensive, or new; who was wild to buy all, could determine on none, and dawdled away her time in rapture and indecision." Or the authorial comment after Edward is finally able to engage himself to Elinor: he was "not only in the rapturous profession of the lover, but in the reality of reason and truth, one of the happiest of men." That sentence is not only Johnsonian but thoroughly characteristic of Austen. Throughout her work, the "reality of reason and truth" is always the standard against which unreason and self-deception are revealed for what they are, offering the only secure ground for the "rapturous professions" of the lover.

The stylistic and emotional range of *Sense and Sensibility* is probably wider than in any other Austen novel, from Johnsonian dignity to the homely colloquialism of Mrs. Jennings, as she describes for Colonel Brandon the emptiness of life after Elinor and Marianne are gone: "how forlorn we shall be . . . Lord! we shall sit and gape at one another as dull as two cats." And Mrs. Jennings herself – a "fat, elderly woman, who talked a great deal, seemed very happy, and rather vulgar" – seems farther down the social scale than any other significant character in Austen's work.

Sense and Sensibility is both the most passionate and the most introspective of Austen's novels. Elinor's relentless self-examination anticipates the Victorian novel, while the witty dialogue that for many readers is Austen's greatest charm is absent here. Even its two heroines seem limited by the requirements of the title. Although *Pride and Prejudice* is similarly titled, Darcy is not always proud, Elizabeth not always prejudiced. With its assortment of grotesques and the harshness of its satire, *Sense and Sensibility* suggests a direction that Austen chose not to follow in her later work.

Certainly it would be a serious misreading to suppose that *Sense and Sensibility* endorses the limitations of commonplace social life. In no other Austen novel are these limitations demonstrated more tellingly, almost cynically, than, for example, in the description of the hospitality offered by the Middletons: "That kind of intimacy must be submitted to which consists of sitting an hour or two together in the same room almost every day. Sir John could do no more, but he did not know that any more was required." The utter incomprehension of the intelligent by the stupid is made apparent when Marianne asks for information about Willoughby – what are "his pursuits, his talents and genius?" – and Sir John can only reply that Willoughby "is a pleasant good-humoured fellow [he is not], and has got the nicest little black bitch of a pointer I ever saw." ("The Middletons and the Palmers – how am I to bear their pity!" exclaims Marianne, after Willoughby's betrayal.)

Sense and Sensibility demonstrates the tyranny of stupidity, the suffering that it imposes on the intelligent and the sensitive. Life for them, in effect, becomes a kind of martyrdom – particularly for Elinor, who cannot escape by transferring social responsibilities to someone else, as Marianne does. The almost cynical realism of the novel can be disconcerting; a large part of everyday social intercourse, we are told, seems to consist of "telling lies when politeness required it" – a task that of course falls on Elinor. The myth of "gentle Jane" could never have originated with anyone who had carefully read *Sense and Sensibility* it may be – nobody's favorite among Austen's novels – this powerful though radically imperfect work abundantly rewards the reader, often in unexpected ways.

Chapter Four

Pride and Prejudice

"It is a truth universally acknowledged, that a single man in posses-
sion of a good fortune, must be in want of a wife."[1] That memorable
opening sentence seems to come from a remote past, from an age
that believed in universal truths and had no hesitation in pronounc-
ing them. Instantly, it dates the novel that it commences. But anticlimax immediately follows. After that portentous introduction, instead of hearing some statement of profound and universal significance, we are solemnly informed that when such a man appears, he
is considered by the local families "as the rightful property of some
one or other of their daughters." Do the single men agree? The question appears to be irrelevant. Certainly it is for Mrs. Bennet, the
mother of at least three marriageable daughters who is eager to find
husbands for them.

In fact, this universal "truth" seems to be recognized only by
matchmaking parents, and that opening ridicules by anticlimax the
neoclassic fondness for such resounding generalizations. Matchmaking parents such as Mrs. Bennet may believe it, but the single
men surely do not, and neither does her daughter Elizabeth, who
does not deal in universal truths. Instead, she is continually shown
gathering and assessing evidence, probing for the truth and finding
it – the truth about Mr. Collins (he is a fool), about Lady Catherine
(she is another), about Mr. Wickham (a more difficult question), and
about Mr. Darcy (the most difficult question of all).

In the three pages of uninterrupted and highly entertaining dialogue between husband and wife that make up the rest of the opening chapter – a striking technical innovation – the reader learns the
essential facts about the Bennet family. There are at least three marriageable daughters, and Lizzy is her father's favorite (but not her
mother's) because she "has something more of quickness than her
sisters." Mr. Bennet is intelligent, satirical, and detached. Mrs. Bennet is vain – "I certainly *have* had my share of beauty" etc. – and

silly as well. The newcomer's name is "Bingley," and he indeed has a "good fortune," "four or five thousand a year," says Mrs. Bennet. In this society, everyone appears to know everyone else's income.

We learn a good deal as well about Mr. and Mrs. Bennet and their marriage. He is always teasing and ridiculing her, offering to send the newcomer "a few lines of my hearty consent" to his marrying any of the Bennet daughters, inquiring whether marrying one of them "was part of his design in settling here." Clearly, this is a loveless marriage. She is foolish and narrow-minded, as her husband realizes, and a hypochondriac as well, with endless complaints about her "poor nerves." Mr. Bennet despises his wife (concealing the fact from her with his formulaic "my dears"), in effect denying her identity and delighting in ridiculing her or in provoking her into fresh displays of stupidity. But *all* parental marriages in Austen's novels appear to be, or to have been, unequal, in the sense that one partner is intellectually inferior to the other, and are, or have been, unhappy. (The possible exception is *Mansfield Park*. Sir Thomas may recognize his wife's limitations, but he invariably treats her with grave decorum.) Such relationships do not, however, distinguish Austen's novels. They are almost a fictional convention – common throughout the eighteenth- and nineteenth-century English novel, whatever may have been the case in society.

The opening chapter ends with a single paragraph of exposition, summing up the relationship between Mr. and Mrs. Bennet. Few novelists have solved the problem of exposition as successfully as Austen does here. She supplies essential information almost entirely through a highly amusing dialogue, creating expectations – which will be fulfilled, in quite unpredictable ways – fully characterizing two of the major figures in the novel (Mr. and Mrs. Bennet) and briefly introducing and distinguishing its two heroines (their daughters Elizabeth and Jane), while indicating that Elizabeth will have the primary role. The character of Mrs. Bennet is summed up in the last three sentences: "She was a woman of mean understanding, little information. When she was discontented, she fancied herself nervous. The business of her life was to get her daughters married; its solace was visiting and news." Those sentences convince because her own words have already demonstrated their truth. And that is all we know or need to know about her. She will amuse us throughout the novel, displaying those qualities and that narrow range of interests in varying, often highly inappropriate contexts.

Mr. Bennet is shown principally as husband in this chapter, but also as father, especially in one remark about his daughters: "They have none of them much to recommend them . . . they are all silly and ignorant like other girls." It is a comment that reveals at least as much about him as it does about them. But Mr. Bennet is by no means as simple a character as his wife, and there is more to learn of him than is shown in this chapter. From what we see of him in these opening pages, we might predict his cynical comment on the neighborhood's reaction to Lydia's elopement – "For what do we live but to make sport for our neighbors and to laugh at them in our turn?" – but not the bitter self-knowledge momentarily revealed when Elizabeth remarks that he "must not be too severe" upon himself: "No, Lizzy, let me once in my life feel how much I have been to blame. I am not afraid of being overpowered by the impression. It will pass away soon enough."

No doubt it would be a considerable exaggeration to say that *Pride and Prejudice* is everyone's favorite novel – after all, Austen is far from being everyone's favorite novelist. To say that Elizabeth Bennet is everyone's favorite heroine might not seem quite so reckless, while to claim that Elizabeth is everyone's favorite *Austen* heroine seems undeniably true. If *Pride and Prejudice* is the most often reprinted, the most widely read, and surely the most often reread of Austen's novels, the explanation can be found principally in the characterization of Elizabeth. Generation after generation of readers have been fascinated by her wit, her independence, her resilience – Elizabeth can love, but she is not a heroine who would ever die of love (as Marianne Dashwood nearly does in *Sense and Sensibility*), or who would suffer silently, as we can imagine her sister Jane doing if Bingley, the man she hoped to marry, had not returned. Unsurprisingly, there have been many imitations of *Pride and Prejudice* – unsurprisingly again, none of them has succeeded. (Austen herself may have been influenced by the example of Beatrice and Benedick, the quarrelling lovers in Shakespeare's *Much Ado about Nothing*.)

Elizabeth charmed her creator as well as the public: "I think her as delightful a creature as ever appeared in print," Austen called her, in a letter of 1813, adding "how I shall be able to tolerate those who do not like *her* at least I do not know" (*Letters*, 296). And on learning that a favorite niece had praised the hero and heroine, Austen remarked that "her liking of Elizabeth and Darcy is enough, she might hate all the others if she would."[2] (No other readers have recorded feeling such enthusiasm for Darcy.) Indeed, for her author as well as for many readers, Elizabeth, and even characters associated with her, seem to have gained an identity outside the novel. On visiting an art exhibit in London, Austen was particularly pleased, she wrote to her sister, at finding "a small portrait of Mrs. Bingley [Jane], excessively like her," adding "I went in hopes of seeing one of her Sister, although there was no Mrs. Darcy," although there were hopes of finding her at the "Great Exhibition." Jane was shown dressed in white, "with green ornaments – which convinces me of what I had always supposed, that green was a favorite color with her." As for Elizabeth, when found "I dare say she will be in yellow."[3]

In Elizabeth and Jane we find again the device of the contrasting sisters, which had worked so effectively in *Sense and Sensibility*. With, of course, important variations – for all of her apparently narrow range, Austen does not repeat herself. Clearly, Elizabeth dominates her own novel, with Jane kept firmly in a secondary position. A simpler and less expressive character than Elizabeth, Jane is inherently less interesting, never threatening to usurp the reader's primary interest as Marianne does in *Sense and Sensibility*. It is Elizabeth's feelings that we are told of or that she herself reveals, and that we are primarily concerned with throughout. On the whole, in Austen's novels, complexity is both more interesting and more admirable than simplicity.

Jane is "steady," she is "amiable," and her most conspicuous quality is her "candour." The moral vocabulary has changed over 200 years; in common usage at least, "amiable" has lost most of its force, meaning no more than "friendly" or "sociable." But in Austen's novels a stronger meaning survives – "loving," or "deserving to be loved," and both meanings certainly apply to Jane. Clearly, though, amiability is not the highest of virtues. It implies a soft and yielding character; Elizabeth can love and is loved, but she is decidedly not "amiable." But Jane's principal virtue, which of course contributes to her amiability, is her "candour," resembling

Elinor's in *Sense and Sensibility* but more extreme, sometimes ignoring reality to put a favorable interpretation on other people's behavior. It can amount to credulity, or even to a willed blindness to reality. Jane's natural, almost instinctive goodness contrasts sharply with Elizabeth's careful examination of motive, in herself and others. And while Jane's love for Bingley may be sincere and faithful, the greater complexity of Elizabeth's feelings makes her love not only more interesting but in a sense more admirable. Jane displays her "candour" by accepting the intermittent "friendship" of the Bingley sisters – "very fine ladies, proud and conceited," Austen has told us – at face value to the last possible moment, and then by excusing their unkindness on grounds of their concern for their brother's welfare. Elizabeth's judgment, that they are proud and snobbish, is clearly more accurate, and such perceptiveness appears more desirable than Jane's almost willed blindness to reality.

Pride and Prejudice contains three distinct varieties of ladies: the "great lady," Lady Catherine de Bourgh; "fine ladies," the Bingley sisters; and simple "ladies," Elizabeth and Jane, who in fact seem to be the only true "ladies" in the novel. The term was ambiguous even in Austen's day, sometimes referring to polite, refined behavior ("ladylike"), sometimes to any woman born to wealth or social position, and sometimes, as apparently with Lady Catherine, to a woman who was either the daughter or the wife of a member of the nobility.

Jane's "candour" is at fault again when she argues that Wickham's willingness to marry Lydia shows that he is "come to a right way thinking," that their "mutual affection will steady them," and that they may "live in so rational a manner" as to make all "past imprudence forgotten." She is clearly talking nonsense, and Elizabeth must point out that these hopes are impossibilities: "Their conduct has been such as neither you nor I, nor any body, can ever forget."

Jane convinces when she is present, either in person or in her sister's thoughts; she has her own happy ending (although not through her own initiative), but for the greater part of the novel, readers never think of her. (No interior view of Jane is ever given, she is seen always through Elizabeth's eyes.) She is, nevertheless, essential. Her character sets off Elizabeth's, her relation to Bingley is intertwined with the central relationship between Elizabeth and Darcy and powerfully influences the plot. Darcy's part in separating Jane and Bingley is one of the major charges that Elizabeth brings against him in refusing his proposal, and Bingley's long-delayed proposal to Jane – clearly encouraged by Darcy – signals the impending engagement between the primary heroine and hero. As for Bingley, he is the perfect match for Jane, and his gregarious, easy-going nature contrasts almost as sharply with Darcy's pride and reserve as Jane's candour does with Elizabeth's satirical wit. (Almost, because Darcy is not characterized as completely or as clearly as Elizabeth, and is simply absent for much of the book.)

The problem with Austen's presentation of Darcy is not that the characterization seems vague and shadowy, as that of Edward Ferrars does in *Sense and Sensibility* – on the contrary, Darcy makes a powerful impression whenever he is present – but that it appears incomplete and inconsistent. Elizabeth is eventually proven very wrong in her hasty judgment of him, but there is considerable justification for her error – which readers are likely to share in, since *Pride and Prejudice*, after the opening chapters, is narrated principally from Elizabeth's point of view. The friendly, hospitable Darcy who greets Elizabeth and the Gardiners at Pemberley is hardly recognizable as the Darcy of the first two volumes. The author's intention seems clear, and evidence is provided that might have led both the heroine and readers to a different opinion of Darcy, but the intention is not fully realized. Nevertheless, he convinces sufficiently. The powerful effect created in the early scenes of the novel carries him through. His arrogance at the neighborhood ball is unforgettable, when he contemptuously remarks, in answer to Bingley's suggestion that he should dance with Elizabeth, "She is tolerable, but not handsome enough to tempt *me*." And Mrs. Bennet's loud dislike for him – "a most disagreeable, horrid man, not at all worth pleasing" – might warn us against jumping to conclusions, or relying too much on "first impressions," to use Austen's words. Mrs. Bennet, after all, is much more likely to be wrong than right. But Elizabeth also can be guilty of prejudice and consequent misjudgment, as she is in her initial view of Darcy, and it is part of her humiliation, when she is forced to change her view, to recognize that in this case she had been as blind as her mother.

Darcy's arrogance continues – notably in his crushing reply to that harmless bore, Sir William Lucas, when Sir William praises dancing as "one of the first refinements of polished societies." "Certainly, Sir; – and it has the advantage also of being in vogue among the less polished societies of the world. – Every savage can dance." But he becomes both more complex and more sympathetic in the Netherfield scenes as Jane lies sick and Elizabeth tends her, as we simultaneously see him rejecting Miss Bingley's obsequious flattery and recognize his growing admiration of Elizabeth's independence. It is Darcy's appreciation of her that begins to alter the reader's attitude toward him. The attraction of course remains onesided. Nothing has yet shaken Elizabeth's prejudice. She "could not help observing . . . how frequently Mr. Darcy's eyes were fixed upon her," but she believes she remains indifferent to him. Yet readers will recognize that she is not as indifferent as she imagines. She is observing him with almost as much interest as he takes in her.

From the beginning of her visit to Netherfield, Darcy's attitude toward Elizabeth contrasts sharply with that of Bingley's sisters. To them, her unconventional response to the news of her sister's illness – "crossing field after field at a quick pace, jumping over stiles and springing over puddles" and finally arriving at Netherfield "with weary ancles [*sic*], dirty stockings, and a face glowing with the warmth of exercise" – seems obviously unladylike. (Elizabeth's energy, both physical and intellectual, is a major source of her charm for readers.) This exaggerated sense of propriety, here and likewise in the case of Mrs. Elton in *Emma*, is shown to originate in a basic feeling of social insecurity – the Bingley fortune is only one generation old and was earned in "trade" – that is, in business.

Darcy's response to Elizabeth's unconventionality is complex, "divided between the admiration of the brilliancy which exercise had given to her complexion" and doubts about the propriety of her coming so far alone. Ironically, the disparaging observations of one of Bingley's sisters – "Her hair so untidy, so blowsy!" and "her petticoat, six inches deep in mud," and the unfeeling comment, "Why must *she* be scampering about the country, because her sister had a cold?" only increase his interest in Elizabeth, leading to his forthright answer when Miss Bingley slyly observes that "this adventure has rather affected your admiration of her fine eyes." "Not at all," he replies. "They were brightened by the exercise."

The Darcy who reappears at Rosings, in volume 2, seems essentially unchanged, stiff and distant, obviously (as he acknowledges in his letter after Elizabeth's rejection of his proposal) resisting his attraction to her for as long as he can, then reluctantly surrendering to it, as he makes his proposal – in a manner that would almost guarantee rejection even if their previous relationship had been different. But a drastic change of attitude and behavior, even of character, seems to have taken place when he reappears to encounter Elizabeth at Pemberley – and there is the problem. Such a change must be shown, must be dramatized, or it cannot convince.

All of Austen's novels are love stories (although that certainly is not a complete description of any of them), and in a love story there are always barriers to be overcome, even – or especially – when the final outcome is as predictable as in *Pride and Prejudice*. There is the barrier of Elizabeth's strong initial dislike for Darcy, there is the barrier of class distinction – Darcy's doubts about the gentility of Elizabeth's family and relations. Her father, though eccentric, is undeniably a gentleman, by behavior and education as well as by birth and status as a landowner, but her mother hardly seems to be a lady. Her manners are offensive, she has brought up her daughters badly, her relatives – the Gardiners – are in "trade," and in this society (at least for its most conservative members) rent from land appears to be the one socially acceptable source of income. There is also a great difference in fortune between Elizabeth and Darcy. He is rich, the Bennets are not, and the Bennet daughters, if still unmarried, will be left poor at their father's death.

The difference in status between Elizabeth and Darcy, then, is considerable, although it can be overcome. (Except in the prejudiced eyes of the Bingley sisters, she is undeniably a lady, whether her mother is or not.) The fools in *Pride and Prejudice* may seem to provide other barriers, but their primary function is to amuse the reader. Mrs. Bennet and Mr. Collins are the most conspicuous, but the category also includes Sir William Lucas, with his harmless snobbery and endless reminiscences of receiving his knighthood at court, and Mary and Lydia Bennet, the learned fool and the noisy fool (although that description doesn't complete the character of Lydia). Lady Catherine de Bourgh also qualifies, "great lady" though she is, in terms of wealth and status. Fools can be found in every rank.

Fools are amusing because, while they often function as blocking characters, their opposition can never be taken very seriously, and because as a rule their folly is self-made rather than resulting from some congenital deficiency. Even Mrs. Bennet and Mr. Collins have enough intelligence to make themselves at least "respectable," that key word in the social vocabulary of eighteenth- and nineteenth-century England. Whether male or female, the fool is likely to have a monomania, a single, all-engrossing interest – Mrs. Bennet, in marrying her daughters (no matter to whom, whether Bingley and Darcy or the rascally Wickham); Mr. Collins, in pleasing his patron, Lady Catherine; Lady Catherine, in displaying her own greatness.

Mrs. Bennet and Mr. Collins complement each other: while both are self-absorbed and entirely insensitive to others, they are exactly opposite in other respects. She is fretful and nervous and querulous (we hear a great deal from Mrs. Bennet about her nerves, and her normal state of mind is a "querulous serenity," while he is "solemn and slow and heavy." His speech, ponderous and unchanging, is nearly always inappropriate. In telling Elizabeth, "[I] assure you in the most animated language of the violence of my affections," his language reveals that there is no affection at all. And after adding that "to fortune I am perfectly indifferent," Collins demonstrates his minute knowledge of the Bennet finances (he is "well aware" that her father can give her nothing, that "one thousand pounds in the 4 percents" is all that Elizabeth can expect to inherit, and that only at her mother's death.

If an intelligent woman is courted by a fool, how should she respond? The answer is not quite as obvious as it might seem. No rational person, surely, would tolerate Mr. Collins's company for long, yet Charlotte Lucas, "a sensible, intelligent young woman, about twenty-seven," decides to put up with it for life – "Solely," we are told, "from the pure and disinterested desire of an establishment," and a belief that at 27 she cannot expect a more desirable suitor. Knowing that Mr. Collins is "neither sensible nor agreeable," that his company is "irksome," that his love for her is imaginary, Charlotte encourages his proposal, then promptly accepts it. Her reason is made clear (and surely would have been clear to readers of Austen's time without explanation): marriage "was the only honorable provision for well-educated young women of small fortune," offering them "their pleasantest preservative from want." (The likeliest alternative would be a forced reliance on the grudging support of her relatives, perhaps to be shuttled back and forth among them. The independence and occupation that Austen herself enjoyed resulted from a combination of unusual family circumstance and a unique talent.)

Choosing between Mr. Collins and a probable future of genteel poverty and dependence on the charity of relatives, Charlotte picks Mr. Collins.

As the heroine of Richardson's *Sir Charles Grandison*, a novel that Austen knew almost by heart, asks, what can a woman do when addressed by "a man of inferior talents. Must she throw away her talents? Must she hide her light under a bushel?" Charlotte does just that, and in doing so loses the respect of her closest friend, Elizabeth. But if the alternative is to become a half-comic, half-pathetic "old maid," like Miss Bates in Austen's *Emma*? What would Elizabeth say to that prospect, for herself? Of course, the question never arises, even when she rejects Darcy. Elizabeth in such a role is unthinkable. And it is never quite certain that Charlotte has made a disastrous mistake – she seems happy enough, occasionally embarrassed by her husband but capable of managing him, or keeping him out of sight, when Elizabeth visits them. "Her home and her housekeeping, her parish and her poultry . . . had not yet lost their charms."

That "yet" is suspicious, although there still might be a possibility that Charlotte's choice was at least right for her. But her cynicism is surely meant to be rejected – "Happiness in marriage is entirely a matter of chance . . . it is better to know as little as possible of the defects of the person with whom you are to pass your life." As Elizabeth answers, "You make me laugh. . . but it is not sound." And finally, Elizabeth's judgment seems unanswerable – Mr. Collins is "conceited, pompous, narrow-minded, silly" – and an intelligent woman who accepts him has recklessly violated "principle and integrity." Incidentally, we know that Austen herself, at 27, when faced with such an offer from an unsuitable man (a landowner, a great deal richer than Mr. Collins), behaved first like Charlotte, then like Elizabeth – accepting the proposal, then withdrawing her acceptance the next morning. But the issue remains one of personal responsibility.

The larger question – of whether society must be so ordered that many women can be forced to choose between marriage, particularly "unequal" marriage, and poverty – is never directly raised in Austen's novels (although the plight of the unmarried woman is dramatized in *Emma* in the situation of Miss Bates, who is dependent on the charity of neighbors for most of the comforts of life). But romantic comedy does not generally challenge the existing social order. Austen's heroines, often surpassing the men of the novels with their intelligence, perceptiveness, and judgment, nevertheless accept the existing order of society, apparently with no serious reservations, and with it the existing division of male and female roles.

Totally absorbed in their preoccupations (marrying off her daughters, for Mrs. Bennet, finding a suitable wife and flattering Lady Catherine for Mr. Collins), the fools simply do not understand most of what goes on around them. Lydia's husband, Wickham, is totally worthless, but because he is a husband and he is handsome, Lydia and her mother are, foolishly, entirely satisfied with him. Neither, of course, can fools understand themselves. Mrs. Bennet talks incessantly, but seems not to hear her own voice: "Nobody can tell what I suffer! – But it is always so. Those who do not complain are never pitied." One of the richest comic scenes in any of Austen's novels develops at the Netherfield ball, as Mrs. Bennet loudly boasts to Mrs. Lucas of Jane's impending marriage to Bingley, as Mary sings interminably ("her voice was weak and her manner affected"), then is rudely interrupted by her mother, "To Elizabeth it appeared that had her family made an agreement to expose themselves as much as they could during the course of the evening, it would have been impossible for them to play their parts with more spirit," as they do, to the reader's amusement.

Simultaneously, the relationship between Darcy and Elizabeth becomes more complex, as he displays his interest more openly, inviting her to dance, while her prejudice against him has been intensified by her acceptance of Wickham's story of his own mistreatment by Darcy. (Incidentally, Elizabeth quite forgets Wickham's lie, that he has no fear of meeting Darcy – rather, it is for Darcy to avoid him.) As the ball opens, she not only expects Wickham to be present, she has "prepared in the highest spirits for the conquest of all that remained unsubdued of his heart." Wickham's story is made up at best of half-truths, but his charm and her own prejudice make her credulous, ready to believe the worst of Darcy and therefore ignoring inconsistencies and improbabilities. And Miss Bingley's intervention, "with an expression of civil disdain," against Wickham simply strengthens Elizabeth's prejudice in his favor. (Miss Bingley knows nothing of the actual relationship between Darcy and Wickham; she has no case against him, except that "considering his descent, one could not expect much better.") Elizabeth's pride is shaken by her experience with Wickham. As she will recognize, she has behaved like a fool, believing what she wants to believe, making no attempt to assess the probabilities of Wickham's account. Darcy's pride, in his social position, will be humbled, but so must hers, in her own powers of perception.

Chapter 18 offers one of the richest comic scenes in Austen's novels – at the same time determining the future action of *Pride and Prejudice* – with almost every one of Elizabeth's relatives (except Jane) playing a ridiculous or humiliating part. Mr. Collins forces himself on Darcy's attention, to Darcy's astonishment and disdain; meanwhile, Mrs. Bennet carries on a monologue with Lady Lucas about Jane's impending marriage to Bingley: "It was . . . such a promising thing for her younger daughters, as Jane's marrying so greatly must throw them in the way of other rich men," etc. Darcy overhears everything, even Mrs. Bennet's irritable reply when Elizabeth cautions her: "What is Mr. Darcy to me, pray, that I should be afraid of him?"

This outburst of vanity has unexpected consequences; overhearing it, Darcy is moved to rescue his friend Bingley from what seems a highly imprudent marriage, just as Jane's happiness appears secure. Meanwhile Mary, who has no musical talent, bores the company with her singing until her father rudely cuts her off. Readers are amused, Elizabeth is humiliated, Darcy's distaste for her low connections is increased, and the immediate consequence is that he takes action to prevent his friend Bingley from marrying Jane.

While Mrs. Bennet is the unwitting temporary block to the marriage between Jane and Bingley, Lady Catherine, another fool, hopes to block any chance of marriage between Elizabeth and Darcy. In doing so, she unwittingly helps to bring it about. Lady Catherine has the habit of interfering in everything, "scolding the villagers into harmony," condescending to all the world. Her similarity to Darcy is plain – like him, she is proud, but her pride is so unreasonable, so absurd, that his own seems more acceptable in comparison. In fact, she actually serves the purpose of putting Elizabeth on a more equal footing with Darcy by giving him a relative he can be ashamed of.

Only the other fools of the novel defer to what Elizabeth calls "the mere greatness of money and rank" – as demonstrated by the card game at Rosings, with Lady Catherine "stating the mistakes of the three others, or relating some anecdotes of herself," Mr. Collins thanking her for the tricks he takes "and apologising if he thought he won too many," while Sir William Lucas, Charlotte's father, is too busy "storing his memory with anecdotes and noble names" to say anything. And as the party concludes, both Lady Catherine and her sycophants are made utterly absurd as they gather about the fire to hear her "determine what weather they were to have on the morrow." A fool herself, she is admired and deferred to only by other fools.

Elizabeth's most striking qualities are her freely displayed wit and independence, and she is never more attractive to readers than when asserting herself against the overbearing Lady Catherine, whether in refusing to give her age when it is demanded or in arguing that younger sisters should not have to wait until their older sisters are married before being allowed into society. " 'Upon my word,' said her Ladyship, 'you give your opinion very decidedly for so young a person.' " In the company at Rosings, it is Elizabeth alone who realizes what should be obvious – that there are no "extraordinary talents or miraculous virtue" to be found in Lady Catherine.

The most conspicuous blocking character in *Pride and Prejudice* is Wickham, the antihero, whose elopement with Lydia Bennet seems to Elizabeth to destroy any chance of a reconciliation with Darcy. Here the alteration of moral standards over nearly 200 years makes it nearly impossible for present-day readers to share in the narrator's outrage; after all, the elopement has Lydia's enthusiastic consent. Wickham becomes a melodramatic "villain," a figure thoroughly out place in the comic world of *Pride and Prejudice*.

But while Wickham proves to be a scoundrel, at first sight "he wanted only regimentals [military uniform] to make him completely charming." (Masculine charm is a suspect quality in Austen's novels; heroes never possess it, antiheroes invariably do.) In his manners he is the opposite of Darcy, displaying "a pleasing address" and "a happy readiness of conversation" in contrast to Darcy's aristocratic reserve. "We neither of us perform for strangers," Darcy remarks to Elizabeth, but Wickham's existence seems to be made up of performances for strangers. He appears to be entirely open and unreserved – again the opposite of Darcy. He readily recites his life story and his grievances to Elizabeth as soon as he is sure of her dis-

like for Darcy. (And Elizabeth's brief attraction to him proves her
own fallibility: "there was truth in his looks," she feels.) But while
Wickham shares his basic insincerity with the other antiheroes, his
impudence – an almost unshakeable assurance under any circumstances – is unique. After he has eloped with Lydia, then been paid
to marry her, and when he knows that Elizabeth is fully aware of his
past of gambling and sexual license, he can say to her that he should
have been delighted to become a country parson, peacefully making
sermons.

The Austen antihero is exactly what the name suggests – he is
not only opposed to the hero's interest (a rival for the heroine's
love, or at least for her hand in marriage), but he is also the opposite
of the hero. And so as the dashing, impetuous Willoughby, impatient
in everything, had been the opposite of the passive, long-suffering
Edward Ferrars and of Colonel Brandon, so Wickham, infinitely
adaptable, insinuating himself into people's confidence with his lies
and his ingratiating manners, is the opposite of Darcy – always himself (sometimes to the point of rudeness), regardless of company or
circumstances.

In himself, Wickham is a good deal less interesting than
Willoughby, but his role in *Pride and Prejudice* is essential. His story
and his charm convince Elizabeth that he has been wronged, and
strengthen her prejudice against Darcy. Her own pride in her discernment is badly shaken when she learns the truth, preparing readers for her reversal of attitude: "of neither Darcy nor Wickham could
she think without feeling that she had been blind, partial, prejudiced, absurd." Yet while Wickham is undeniably a heartless, hypo-
critical scoundrel and shows no sign of reformation, in the comic
world of *Pride and Prejudice* the worst punishment that is awarded
is simply for him to remain himself (just as the fools must do),
spending more than his income, sponging off Elizabeth and the Bin-
gleys whenever he can.

Pride and Prejudice – the title follows the form of *Sense and Sensibility*. Austen would never use such a dichotomy again. (Very likely it
was inspired by a passage in Fanny Burney's *Cecilia*, summing up the
events of that novel: "The whole of this unfortunate business . . . has
been the result of PRIDE AND PREJUDICE.") Pride and prejudice, sense
and sensibility – modern readers are likely to think that this use of

contrasting moral qualities to provide titles was a characteristic of the time, but it was not. Novels occasionally took their titles from a single quality – *Discipline*, *Self-Control*, or Austen's own *Persuasion* – more often from a place, as in Austen's *Mansfield Park*. But before Austen's day, and long afterwards, they were most commonly named for their principal character – *Robinson Crusoe*, *Tom Jones*, *Sir Charles Grandison*, *Ivanhoe*, *David Copperfield*, *Jane Eyre*, and Austen's own *Emma*.

Austen's original title, "First Impressions," seems appropriate enough, but quite lacks the resonance, the multiple implications of *Pride and Prejudice*. This final title is distinctive, memorable, and accurate, provided that readers recognize that both hero and heroine are proud and that both are prejudiced. There are of course differences between them. Elizabeth's pride is personal – for qualities she knows she possesses; Darcy's pride in considerable part is simply a pride in status and possessions, and to that extent is indistinguishable from Lady Catherine's. Darcy can also, we discover, take a more justifiable pride in his performance of all the responsibilities that ownership of Pemberley entails. (Elizabeth's opinion of him is considerably improved by the favorable testimony of his housekeeper on Darcy's qualities as an employer.)

In its organization, *Pride and Prejudice*, unlike *Northanger Abbey*, follows the common three-volume form. (Since *Pride and Prejudice* is a novel of only moderate length, these volumes are extremely short.) Modern reprints more often than not ignore the original division, numbering the chapters consecutively from beginning to end. But Austen was aware of this traditional requirement, and the plot development of *Pride and Prejudice* suggests that she took its logic into account. The conclusion of volume 1, at the end of chapter 23, is a characteristic dialogue between Mr. and Mrs. Bennet concerning Mr. Collins (who has just become engaged to Charlotte Lucas), while volume 2 opens with the news that Bingley and his sisters will not be returning to Highbury, and consequently that "Hope was over, entirely over" for Jane, and closes with, "To Pemberley, therefore, they were to go" – clearly foreshadowing Elizabeth's encounter there with Darcy.

With that, the novel enters a new phase, as the scene of action moves to Hunsford (the location of Mr. Collins's rectory) and Rosings (Lady Catherine's estate), reuniting Darcy and Elizabeth (to Elizabeth's surprise), then apparently separating them forever after her angry rejection of his proposal – a proposal appropriate to the arrogant, self-confident character the novel has presented up to this point. But it is Darcy's letter, or rather Elizabeth's response to it, that marks the turning-point of the novel. Elizabeth, then, must review and correct her judgment of both Darcy and of Wickham – a process shared by the reader, who has also been mistaken.

The inevitable union of heroine and hero is clearly in sight as the Gardiners take Elizabeth with them to the north, and as she reluctantly accepts her aunt's suggestion of visiting Darcy's estate, when it appears that he is away. "To Pemberley, therefore, they were to go," and every reader can foresee the outcome of that visit. But the turning point of the novel has already been passed – marked not by a dramatic scene but by Elizabeth's painful self-analysis, after reading Darcy's letter, ending in her conclusion that "Of neither Darcy, nor Wickham, could she think, without feeling that she had been blind, partial, prejudiced, absurd."

But it is too early for happiness. There are pages to be filled, and the ending must not seem too quick or too easy. Just as Elizabeth realizes that it is a changed Darcy she has met at Pemberley, a Darcy who has taken her rebuke to heart, and that it depends only on her to encourage him and "bring on the renewal of his addresses," the news comes of Wickham's elopement with Lydia. The elopement is adequately motivated – it seems credible that the Wickham and the Lydia who have been presented might commit such an act – but to many readers it seriously weakens the final volume, offering too sudden and drastic a change in tone.

Comedy survives, to be sure – in Mrs. Bennet's anxieties (if Mr. Bennet comes home, "Who is to fight Wickham, and make him marry her?" [Lydia]), in Mary's moralizing ("Unhappy as the event must be for Lydia, we may draw from it this useful lesson; that one false step involves her in endless ruin"), in the sympathy of Mr. Collins ("The death of your daughter would have been a blessing in comparison of this"), and in the opinion of Lady Catherine (after such a disgraceful event, "who . . . will connect themselves with such a family?"). And

Mr. Bennet, after briefly feeling an uncharacteristic sense of bitter guilt, returns to his ironic stance: "For what do we live but to provide sport for our neighbors and laugh at them in our turn?" The narrator's comment on the reaction of neighbors to the whole event is as cynical as Mr. Bennet's: "It would have been more for the advantage of conversation, had Miss Lydia Bennet come upon the town" (become a prostitute), but "with such an husband, her misery was considered certain." Mrs. Bennet is at her most absurd throughout, particularly in her eagerness to carry the good news that Lydia is actually married (to a scoundrel) to the entire neighborhood. Lydia, meanwhile – noisy, fearless, unabashed and untamable ("We were so merry all the way home! We talked and laughed so loud, that any body might have heard us ten miles off!") – becomes almost an archetypal figure of the uncontrollable adolescent.

The elopement has been prepared for to some extent. The issue, as Austen proposes it, is moral. Lydia is held responsible for her own fate, even though (as Mr. Bennet is honest enough to recognize) her parents can be held responsible for her faulty education. The actual events seem appropriate to the characters involved. Lydia must and will have a man – that has been thoroughly established – and there is no strain on the reader's credulity in supposing that Wickham, fleeing from his debts, would prefer to escape with female company. And on the whole, Austen handles the affair with restraint and with humor whenever possible. The problem is simply that, with Wickham becoming that stereotype of eighteenth-century fiction, the heartless seducer, the episode is so thoroughly incongruous. It seems to belong to another and much less interesting, novel.

With Lydia married to Wickham and her (and her family's) reputation at least partially salvaged, Elizabeth must become engaged to Darcy. But how is this inevitable outcome to be brought about? Quite unpredictably, by a fine comic device, the appearance of Lady Catherine to demand a public denial from Elizabeth of this so far nonexistent engagement. That she should condescend to visit the Bennets amazes Elizabeth and promptly arouses the reader's curiosity. The scene is highly satisfying – the arrogant, overbearing Lady Catherine is at last openly confronted and defeated, first by Elizabeth's cool logic (she will not be kept from marrying Darcy "by knowing that his mother and aunt [Lady Catherine] wished him to marry Miss De Bourgh," since "you both did all you could in planning the marriage"), then by her spirited self-assertion: "Neither duty, nor honour, nor gratitude" would be violated by her marriage to Darcy, and "the resentment of his family . . . would not give me one moment's concern."

Lady Catherine's defeat is made total when her report of the interview convinces Darcy that Elizabeth loves him and encourages him to make a second proposal. The ironic verdict on her meddling is pronounced by Elizabeth: "Lady Catherine has been of infinite use, which ought to make her happy, for she loves to be of use." And so the novel moves quickly to its conclusion. Jane must still be matched with Bingley, but that outcome follows almost automatically. Sentimentality is avoided – "Happy for all her maternal feelings was the day on which Mrs. Bennet got rid of her two most deserving daughters." (In which the unexpectedly colloquial "got rid of" exactly describes her maternal feelings.)

The "failure" of the third volume can be summed up simply – on the whole, it is less entertaining than the first two. But to say that is far from condemning it entirely: few novels by any writer have been as entertaining. And volume 3 certainly contains its own good things – conspicuously, Elizabeth's final interview with Lady Catherine, but also her continuing wit and independence ("What are men to rocks and mountains?"), Mr. Bennet's irony, and Mrs. Bennet's splendid foolishness: "Three daughters married! Ten thousand a year . . . . I shall go distracted!"

A fairy-tale ending it has seemed to some readers, and in a sense it is, but set in a recognizable time and place. The Cinderella motif is clear. But to admit this quality, this element of fantasy, is not to condemn – art surely exists in part to satisfy human desire where life cannot. While pure fantasy would be inappropriate, here it is disguised, made acceptable by realistic detail. Ideologically inclined readers may find in this conclusion a concession to male dominance and the social command that women *must* marry. But there is no reason to believe that Elizabeth will be any more submissive in marriage than during Darcy's courtship. (We are told that, after the wedding, Darcy's young sister is astonished, almost alarmed, by Elizabeth's "lively, sportive manner" of talking to her husband.) In any case, as Marilyn Butler remarks, "There is no reason why we should object that it [*Pride and Prejudice*] clear message; it has been compared with Mozart, who has no message either" (Butler, 134).

Chapter Five

Mansfield Park

"All who think deeply & feel much will give the preference to Mansfield Park," observed one early admirer, but readers in general have not agreed. "We do not think it as a *whole* equal to P.&P [*sic*]"; "Not so clever as *Pride and Prejudice;*" "Not liked it near so well as P.&P." So read the first three of a collection of comments on *Mansfield Park* by contemporary readers, gathered for the author by relatives and friends.[1] Readers who praised *Mansfield Park* found other reasons than its heroine for their admiration – its realism (the characters seemed drawn from "nature"), its good sense ("the most sensible novel" she had ever read, said one), its "moral tendency."

Even Austen's devoted sister, Cassandra, thought the new novel "quite as clever" but "not so brilliant" as *Pride and Prejudice*. That "brilliant" no doubt refers especially to the wit and vigor of the dialogue, above all to Elizabeth's speeches, while "clever" may describe the plotting and characterizations of both novels. The difference that readers have always sensed lies primarily in the contrast between the two heroines, Elizabeth Bennet and Fanny Price. Elizabeth is overflowing with energy, both intellectually and physically; she seems continually in motion; she responds to attractive men – not only Darcy but Wickham and Colonel Fitzwilliam. Fanny, in contrast, appears debilitated, almost sickly – one reason for the oddly Victorian flavor that *Mansfield Park* occasionally displays. She is never given a witty remark. She is tired even by short walks, and she leaves Mansfield Park only twice during the novel – for the excursion to Sotherton, 14 miles away, and the visit to her mother in Portsmouth. But Fanny is a Christian heroine, and literary tradition required that such heroines should be shown as not quite at home in this world, and often not destined for a long stay in it.

But Fanny's role is not simply that of the poor relation who finally marries the younger son of the great house. She becomes, in a way that no other Austen heroine does, the guardian of morality and principle in her world, not only behaving well herself under all circumstances but observing and judging the behavior of others. It is an ungrateful role, almost necessarily making her appear censorious and superior. "The most terrible incarnation we have of the female prig-pharisee," one twentieth-century critic called her, referring to her "cast-iron self-righteousness and steely rigidity of prejudice."[2] Even C. S. Lewis, a critic who strongly approves of the moral scheme of *Mansfield Park*, with its religious implications, observes of Fanny that she has "nothing except rectitude of mind; neither passion, nor physical courage, nor wit, nor resource."[3]

Pride and Prejudice opens with a chapter of lively dialogue, contrasting Mrs. Bennet's apparently absurd hopes of matrimony for her daughters (hopes that are in fact realized) with her husband's ironic responses. *Mansfield Park* commences with a sober exposition of family history: "About thirty years ago, Miss Maria Ward of Huntingdon, with only seven thousand pounds, had the good luck to captivate Sir Thomas Bertram of Mansfield Park."[4] Except for the telling phrase, "had the good luck," that sentence might have been written by almost any English novelist of the time. But Austen's characteristic irony is soon evident: "All Huntingdon exclaimed on the greatness of the match, and her uncle, the lawyer, himself allowed her to be at least three thousand pounds short of any equitable claim to it." Marriage seen as a market place, in which the cash value of each party can be calculated exactly and a "great match" has nothing to do with marital happiness – this traditional attitude is a reality with which every Austen heroine except Emma Woodhouse must cope. A possible consequence of such matches is dramatized in the disastrous marriage of Rushworth and Maria in *Mansfield Park*.

Sir Thomas, Lady Bertram, and her sister Mrs. Norris are all characterized as they consider Mrs. Norris's proposal to aid her other sister, Mrs. Price (who has a large family, an invalid husband, and a small income). They are one-dimensional characters, essentially fixed and unchanging – as Austen's parental figures generally are. Mrs. Norris at first appears to be a familiar comic type, pretending to virtues that she does not have – making an apparently generous offer to help her sister, Mrs. Price, by bringing up one of her daughters, then transferring the trouble and responsibility of raising the girl to Sir Thomas, even though she herself is a childless widow with a comfortable income. But she is no simple hypocrite, that stock figure of comedy. She "might so little know herself," Austen comments, "as to walk home . . . after this conversation, in the happy belief of being the most liberal-minded sister and aunt in the world."

Lady Bertram, who seems almost an allegorical figure – Indolence personified – says little and does nothing throughout the novel, but when she speaks it can be very much to the point. When Mrs. Norris volubly explains why she cannot be expected to take any responsibility – " 'Then she had better come to us,' said Lady Bertram with the utmost composure." Sir Thomas displays his characteristic deliberation as he considers all the possibilities involved in such an action – even the need to provide for this girl in case, when she grows up, she cannot find a husband. But deliberation is not necessarily wisdom. When he comments on the distinction that must always be made between the newcomer and his own daughters, he is clearly asking for the impossible: not only must Fanny be continually reminded "that she is not a Miss Bertram," but it will be necessary "to preserve in the minds of my *daughters* the consciousness of what they are, without making them think too lowly of their cousin."

Readers have been told nothing more of Fanny than her age (she is 10 when she arrives at Mansfield), but just as one could safely guess after reading the first chapter of *Pride and Prejudice* that it would be mainly concerned with the marrying of Elizabeth Bennet, so the opening chapter of *Mansfield Park* not only indicates unmistakably that Fanny is to become the heroine but implies that she will finally marry one of Sir Thomas's two sons, as romance traditionally requires. What cannot be foreseen is more significant – that Fanny, not Sir Thomas or any of his children – will become the moral guardian of Mansfield, not so much by her actions as by her refusals. Only on rereading (and *Mansfield Park* repays rereading better than any other Austen novel except *Emma*) does the irony in Sir Thomas's declaration that he hopes "there can be nothing to fear" for his daughters from association with Fanny "and everything to hope for from her" become recognizable.

Fanny, then, arrives – a shy and timid girl, befriended only by her cousin Edmund, Sir Thomas's younger son, and constantly persecuted by Mrs. Norris, who makes an admirable wicked stepmother (even if that is not quite her relationship). An ongoing contrast is created between the neglected, often exploited, Fanny and her spoiled and pampered cousins, Julia and Maria Bertram – proud, "accomplished" girls, already promising to be beautiful. Inevitably, the Bertram daughters feel superior to their cousin, not only by right of birth and wealth, but from their superior education: as one of them observes, they can recite "the Roman emperors as low as Severus; besides a great deal of the Heathen Mythology, and all the Metals, Semi-Metals, Planets, and distinguished philosophers," while Fanny does not even know "the principal rivers in Russia."

Yet as *Mansfield Park* will reveal, their education has serious deficiencies – its purpose appears to be simply to increase their marriageability. There is no love of knowledge or of learning for its own sake. As one of them remarks, when reminded by her governess that there is still something for them to learn, "Yes, I know there is, till I am seventeen." And surprisingly, in the home of the conscientious and highly principled Sir Thomas, something of fundamental importance has been overlooked in the upbringing of his daughters. Maria and Julia, "with all their promising talents," nevertheless happen to be "entirely deficient in the less common acquirements of self-knowledge, generosity and humility. In everything but disposition, they were admirably taught."

With the exception of Edmund, the children of the house fail to deserve their birthright – Tom, the older brother, is the archetypal elder son, feeling "born only for expense and enjoyment" – while both parents, as in *Pride and Prejudice*, are inadequate in their different ways. Nevertheless, as Lionel Trilling notes, "of all the fathers of Jane Austen's novels, Sir Thomas is the only one to whom admiration is given."[5] This authorial approval may seem surprising, considering that his older son is a wastrel (until taught seriousness by a dangerous illness), that both of his daughters have acquired manners, rather than principles, and that one, Maria, after an adulterous affair with Henry Crawford, must be expelled from respectable society. He seems even less successful as a parent than Mr. Bennet, but Mr. Bennet, the pure ironist, stands for nothing, while Sir Thomas does, even though he largely fails in his duty as a father.

After a far more leisurely opening than that of *Pride and Prejudice* – three chapters to introduce the Bertram family and allow the heroine to grow up – Sir Thomas departs to attend to his property in the West Indies, relying on the watchfulness of Mrs. Norris and the "good judgment" of Edmund to keep all well at home, since Lady Bertram is clearly useless. It is only in his absence that the real action of the novel can commence, with the engagement of Maria to Mr. Rushworth, instigated by Mrs. Norris, and the arrival of Henry and Mary Crawford and their intimacy with the young Bertrams. Everything that follows will depend on these events.

As the narrator ironically observes, the engagement is "unexceptionable." Maria is beautiful and well-born, and Rushworth has £12,000 a year. It is true that he is also exceedingly stupid ("a heavy young man, with not more than common sense" is Austen's euphemistic description), but no one gives this point any consideration. In fact, nothing is missing in this engagement but love. Rushworth is too limited to feel its lack, while Maria focuses on the material benefits she will gain from the marriage. Rushworth is even richer than her father and will provide her with "the house in town [London]" that she craves. Consequently, it becomes "her evident duty to marry Mr. Rushworth if she could." The absent Sir Thomas, when informed, is "truly happy in the prospect of an alliance so unquestionably advantageous."

"Alliance" is the appropriate term – in the world of *Mansfield Park* a great landowner seems a miniature ruler in his own territory, for whom personal feelings or personal qualities have not much more to do with engagement and marriage than in the case of royalty. A son-in-law as wealthy as Rushworth will substantially increase Sir Thomas's own influence. But while eager to augment the family's wealth and power, Sir Thomas has clearly been derelict in a more important duty – he has somehow failed to transmit to his children the values that could not only make their lives more fulfilling but might justify the privileges to which they have been born.

With the appearance of Henry and Mary Crawford, brother and sister, the cast of characters is nearly complete. Their essential qualities are immediately revealed: "To anything like a permanence of abode, or limitation of society, Henry Crawford had, unluckily, a great dislike," while Mary "would have everybody marry if they can do it properly" – that is, "as soon as they can do it to advantage." Her personal style is the opposite of Sir Thomas's, but her attitude toward marriage is almost identical. It is clear that the newcomers are essentially worldly, concerned with externals. Physical appearance, as usual in Austen's novels, is barely outlined: Mary is "remarkably pretty," Henry "though not handsome, had air and countenance" and "the manners of both were lively and pleasant." In this strongly Tory novel, in which performance of duty is the principal touchstone of character, such manners can appear frivolous and therefore suspicious in themselves. But Henry is more seriously delinquent – by absenting himself from his estate in an endless search for pleasure, he refuses to perform the function required of his class, and in doing so discredits and undermines the social order that privileges him.

But Henry is delinquent in another respect. By his own sister's report, he "is the most horrible flirt that can be imagined," who has already broken hearts. But "flirt" seems far too mild a term for Henry Crawford, and Mary herself is condemned by this casual dismissal of her brother's fault. Henry is a psychological sadist with a devouring egotism, behaving as if he can be convinced of his own reality only by exerting power over others, and finding that the surest proof of power is the infliction of pain. He is a role player (in this resembling Austen's other antiheroes), ever searching for new parts to play while neglecting the social role that he was born to perform. And in courting Fanny, he undertakes what a recent critic calls "the most difficult role of all – the role of sincerity." Predictably, he cannot not sustain it.

Mary, too, is characterized by her casual acceptance of her brother's fault. In her liveliness and wit, she seems at first to resemble Elizabeth Bennet, but with continued reading, and still more with rereading, her insensitivity, her shallow cynicism, her unthinking acceptance of the standards of fashionable London society, her treachery toward Fanny, to whom she pretends friendship – all become too apparent. Mary's style is to be lightly ironic toward society (meaning fashionable London, in her case, with its frivolity and its casual attitude toward sexual morality) in order to establish her own unconventionality, while in fact entirely accepting its standards.

She may resemble Elizabeth Bennet in her liveliness, but not in her use of traditional female wiles, such as a supposedly charming defiance of reason or reality, while her speeches reveal a calculation and a subtle insincerity that's quite lacking in Elizabeth. Mary trades on this stereotype of the irrational female with what Austen calls her "feminine lawlessness" – a willed refusal to accept, for example, the realities of time and distance. "I cannot be dictated to by a watch," she exclaims, when arguing about the distance they have walked. But for the infatuated Edmund, "the greatest degree of rational consistency could not have been more engaging."

Her contempt for Edmund's vocation is simply an unthinking prejudice – Edmund has "lowered" himself by his ordination and by his intention of becoming merely a country clergyman, rather than a fashionable London preacher. Mary's attitude toward both religion and marriage, like her brother's toward his estate, is both morally and socially subversive. Religion in *Mansfield Park* is seen as the basis of morality, and marriage as the foundation of the social order. It should not be surprising that Mary Crawford violates the sanctity of personal relationships as well, first by forcing an intimacy on Fanny, when there is no other company to be had, as Henry seeks to force love, and then by exploiting this relationship to help her brother in his unwelcome courtship. Taking into account the full implications of Mary's words and actions, it becomes possible to accept Austen's summary of her character, with its biblical echoes – "a mind led astray and bewildered, and without any suspicion of being so; darkened, yet fancying itself light."

Much of the major action is now foreseeable: Henry will surely practice his skill at "flirting" with one or both of the Bertram daughters, and Mary will set about husband hunting. These expectations will be satisfied, but in an Austen novel the unexpected is sure to occur as well. And it does, with the worldly Mary Crawford finding herself attracted not to Tom Bertram, the heir to Mansfield (as she had expected), but to Edmund, the younger son, and with Henry falling in love with Fanny, against all apparent likelihood. He intends merely another flirtation, which he will break off at his own pleasure, causing Fanny enough pain to demonstrate his power over her. He would then, no doubt, despise her for her weakness, as he despises Maria and Julia.

His motives change as the game proves more difficult than he had expected and as he senses qualities in Fanny that he himself does not possess and has heretofore not found in a woman – her gentleness, her "strong affections," her "steadiness and regularity of conduct," her "high notion of honour," her unshakeable "faith and integrity." And Mary is drawn to Edmund from this same sense of

qualities lacking in herself. To use the religious phraseology that
seems appropriate to this novel, the Crawfords seek but they cannot
find, because they have blinded themselves to the moral principles
that are the true source of the qualities they desire.

The Sotherton visit is organized by Mrs. Norris – who loves to make
arrangements – and welcomed by almost everyone else, as a relief to
the dullness of Mansfield. But, while this pleasure party offers keen
satisfaction for readers, it produces little pleasure and much vexation
for most of the participants. Its purpose, in theory, is to help Rushworth – who has no taste whatever – plan the proper landscaping
of his estate. Elaborate and costly landscaping of great estates, according to the latest style, was a frequent form of aristocratic display
through much of the eighteenth century, continuing in Austen's day.
In *Mansfield Park*, such disregard for tradition, such concern with
contemporary fashion, regardless of expense, symbolize upper-class
superficiality and irresponsibility. Significantly, it is Henry Crawford
(whose principal concern with his own estate is to spend its rev-
enues) who takes the lead in the enterprise.

But landscaping is quickly forgotten in this pleasure party, which
produces vexation rather than pleasure for most of the participants.
The Bertram daughters are jealous of each other as Crawford carefully divides his attention between them, committing himself to neither. Family disunity is the result, since either Maria or Julia must be
miserable whenever he is present. "Happy Julia! Unhappy Maria!" is
the result when Henry invites Julia to share the driver's box with him
in his light carriage on the way to Sotherton, so that he can offer her
a lesson in driving. And Maria, necessarily, takes her seat inside the
heavy Bertram coach "in gloom and mortification." But Maria will
receive attention once they arrive.

Upon the party's arrival they are greeted by Mr. Rushworth,
Maria's fiancé. The language does not suggest an atmosphere of gai-
ety but rather a forced, mechanical quality: "after the *business* of arriving," was over, it was "first *necessary* to eat" (italics added). The
compulsory tour of the house, with viewing of the family portraits
("no longer anything to anybody but Mrs. Rushworth [Mr. Rushworth's mother]"), bores everyone except the inexperienced Fanny,
and the sophisticated Mary Crawford commits a most revealing blun-
der with her comment, while visiting the antique Sotherton chapel,

that "in those days, I fancy, parsons were very inferior even to what they are now," followed by her observation, on learning that Edmund is to be a clergyman, that "You really are fit for something better. Come, do change your mind. It is not too late." "Something better" – the gap between them that is revealed in that casual phrase proves to be unbridgeable.

The central action of the Sotherton visit takes place, appropriately, in a long continuous scene in the "wilderness" – literally a planted wood of about two acres. The entire scene (certainly one of the most brilliantly executed in any of Austen's novels) is highly theatrical in its technique – in this respect a foreshadowing of the theatricals at Mansfield – as group after group appears, performs, and exits, while Fanny observes. Within this "wilderness," which seems to be moral as well as physical, all but Fanny will be confused and led astray.

Having made their way in through a gate that should have been locked, Edmund and Mary stroll through the wilderness, with Fanny accompanying and observing. With a renewed attack on the ministry, Mary again reveals both her insensitivity and her lack of moral grounding. "A clergyman is nothing," she declares, meaning that the profession has no social prestige, at least in fashionable London. Edmund defends his choice, without effect, but blinds himself to the basic incompatibility between them, and the conversation ends where it began, as all of their conversations on that topic will do. That incompatibility seems plain enough, but the attraction of Mary is overpowering, and the physical contact with her, as Edmund offers her his arm and invites her to lean on it, becomes almost erotic.

It is Maria's turn next to be blinded to reason and morality – much more completely and dangerously than Edmund had been – as she enters the wilderness with Crawford and Rushworth, who is promptly dismissed to find a key to the iron gate at the far end of the wood. With this scene Maria enters a moral wilderness from which she will never escape. Henry Crawford and Maria hint more and more openly at her forthcoming marriage, and Henry indicates his regret, almost offers to help her escape. (But all his speeches are equivocations, implying much while committing him to nothing.) When he observes to Maria, referring to the view beyond the gate, that "You have a very smiling scene before you" – inevitably suggesting her forthcoming marriage – her reply is pathetic: "But unluckily that iron gate, that ha-ha [a ditch surrounding the "wilderness"] give me a feeling of restraint and hardship. I cannot get out, as the starling said."

The reference is to an often-quoted passage in Laurence Sterne's *A Sentimental Journey through England and France*, published in 1768, but before accepting its pathos readers should recollect that Maria has caged herself and could yet escape. Given the chance by her father, she will refuse it. Erotic implications appear, foreshadowing the final catastrophe, in Henry's suggestion that she might "get out without the key and without Mr. Rushworth's authority," simply by going around the edge of the gate, with his own help, provided she could only "think it not prohibited." "Prohibited! Nonsense! I certainly can get out that way and I will" is her answer, and so in effect she finally does, by eloping with Henry hundreds of pages later. Fanny's warning seems even richer in sexual suggestion: "You will certainly hurt yourself against those spikes – you will tear your gown – you will be in danger of slipping into the ha-ha" – symbolic prophecies that will be fulfilled.

This is one of the most remarkable scenes in Austen's novels. The aesthetic effect has been well described by Edmund Wilson in his "A Long Talk about Jane Austen": "the sensations I remember . . . were purely aesthetic ones; a delight in the focusing of the complex group through the ingenuous eyes of Fanny, the balance and harmony of the handling of the contrasting timbres of the characters."[6] Wilson's perception of Austen's method is acute, yet incomplete. No criticism that fails to consider the moral and sexual implications of this whole long scene – Crawford's deceitful tempting of Maria, for example, in which he carefully avoids commitment, and her willed unawareness of his full meaning – and assumes that these implications are unrelated to a purely "aesthetic" effect can fully account for its power.

The lines of action developed at Sotherton – Crawford's flirtation with Maria and her far more serious response, with Rushworth's increasing anger; the growing attraction between Edmund and Mary, with Fanny's pain as she watches helplessly – prepare readers for the amateur theatricals at Mansfield. This brilliant comic sequence, filling the final third of the first volume, shows a sustained power of construction nowhere apparent in *Sense and Sensibility* or even *Pride and Prejudice* combined with a greater psychological acuity than can be found anywhere else in Austen's novels – notably in the willed blindness of Maria to the consequences of her own actions and still more in the motivation of Henry Crawford, driven by an insatiable egotism to demonstrate his power over women.

The play to be performed at Mansfield, *Lovers' Vows*, seems absurd to the modern reader (and clearly seemed so to Austen as well), full of ranting speeches, absurd improbabilities, and melodramatic situations. In its own time, however, it was not only popular but controversial, seeming to replace traditional moral standards with a subversive sentimental ethic in which the rightness of an action depends on the feelings of the performer rather than on religious teachings and established moral rules – a disturbing doctrine to conservative minds, in a revolutionary era. It seems essentially the ethic of sensibility, as expressed by Marianne Dashwood in *Sense and Sensibility*, but applied to more controversial situations – to removing the social stigma from bastardy, for example. And while there may seem to be a touch of snobbery as well in the authorial disapproval – actors were long regarded as rogues or vagabonds and actresses as immoral women – reasons enough for disapproval become apparent in the events themselves.

Austen's amateurs, we are shown, dangerously confuse reality and fiction – their parts in the play with the roles they take, or hope to take, in life. Whether they act their parts well or badly hardly seems to matter to them. At least they exhibit themselves to the utmost. Tom Bertram tries to display his authority as elder son. Edmund reverses himself embarrassingly, after his initial disapproval, by taking the part of Anhalt, Amelia's lover, played by Mary. While convincing himself that he acts out of consideration for Mary – "Consider what it would be to act Amelia with a stranger" – his real motive is clear. He does not want to see her rehearsing love scenes with another man. Henry Crawford requires constant diversion and desires to exhibit his own skill in acting – an ability already apparent in his flirtations with Maria and Julia – and can enjoy the further pleasure of rehearsing a passionate scene of reunion with his long-lost mother, played by Maria, while Julia is bitterly disappointed at not becoming herself the object of Crawford's embraces.

Meanwhile Fanny, as at Sotherton, observes and suffers. But even Fanny, suffering an agony of shyness, is about to be drawn in, when she is saved – most appropriately – by an intensely melodra-

matic *coup de théatre:* "the door of the room was thrown open, and
Julia appearing at it, with a face all aghast, exclaimed, 'My father is
come! He is at the hall at this moment.' " Here the original volume
division counts – much of the effect is lost if Julia's announcement is
not followed by the words "END OF VOL. 1" and a half-page of blank
space.

The return of Sir Thomas signifies an outward and temporary
restoration of authority and order, in place of the selfish and irresponsible egotism that has dominated the actions of everyone except
Fanny during the rehearsal. But the situation remains basically unchanged. Henry and Mary Crawford continue their siege of Mansfield, Henry by turning his attentions to Fanny and even becoming
her suitor, and Mary by doing her best to persuade Edmund to
abandon his vocation, the ministry. Meanwhile, damage has been
done that cannot be repaired. Maria has realized how repulsive
Rushworth is to her, but marries him – ruining her life in doing
so – out of spite and anger against Henry Crawford.

There has been warning of Sir Thomas's coming, which the
characters concerned (and very likely most readers) have forgotten – the letter announcing his hope of soon returning to his
"beloved" family. Maria's response has been to practice a willed
blindness, as Austen explains with grave irony: "Something would
happen to delay him – that favouring *something* which every body
who shuts their eyes while they look, or their understandings while
they reason, feels the comfort of." Maria has refused to use her understanding in other situations as well, both in forming her engagement with Rushworth and in entering an uncertain relationship with
Crawford.

While it might be argued that Maria's engagement has been
"rational" – i.e. calculating – it is in fact highly irrational, because it
ignores the realities of Rushworth's stupidity and of her own feelings. Her recognition of Crawford's treachery leads not to self-
examination and recognition of error but to a determination to
secure Rushworth and his fortune at least. "It was a very proper
wedding . . . the etiquette of the day might stand the strictest inspection" – the opening and conclusion of that paragraph sum up a ceremony containing everything except affection – a fact that remains

unnoticed by those present because the external show is so expensive and so thoroughly proper.

With Maria's marriage, Fanny moves to the center of the novel. Volumes 2 and 3 of *Mansfield Park* present the testing of Fanny. She resists Crawford's vigorous courtship, even when resistance compels her to face the awesome disapproval of Sir Thomas. She becomes an actor, rather than an observer, although the only action possible to her is refusal – but given the circumstances, her totally dependent position, her deep respect for Sir Thomas, the apparent hopelessness of her love for Edmund, that refusal seems almost heroic.

Various events reflect Fanny's improved position. The invitation to dinner at the Grants', the journey there in the Bertram carriage (turned out especially for herself, to Mrs. Norris's consternation), the ball (essentially a coming-out party) that Sir Thomas arranges for her – all signal her change of role. She even becomes pretty, if not actually beautiful. Beauty would be inappropriate to the modest Fanny.

More important, it is Fanny, more than the worldly Sir Thomas, even more than Edmund, who embodies the true spirit of Mansfield Park. Old manners and morals clash with new, country is opposed to town, simplicity to sophistication, seriousness to flippancy and a continual search for diversion. Only religious faith, apparently, can guarantee stability. Consequently, Mary Crawford's unconcealed contempt for the clergy, the proper guardians of the moral and social order (whatever their individual failings), may be more dangerous than her brother's behavior. Ironically, Sir Thomas has managed to impart the moral and religious values he and Mansfield should represent only to his foster child – not at all to his own daughters or his elder son, and only partially to Edmund.

Everything depends on Fanny's insight and courage. Sir Thomas and Edmund are both taken in by the Crawfords; she alone recognizes the seriousness of the threat they pose, having the potential to undermine the fixed principles, the stability and constancy of behavior on which Mansfield depends (and by implication, the entire social order). She must not only resist the courtship of Henry Crawford, to which both her cousins had succumbed, but she must resist it under the most difficult circumstances. Both Sir Thomas – an awe-inspiring figure for her, and one to whom she feels profoundly in-

debted – and Edmund, whom she loves, urge her to accept Crawford. Worse still, Edmund is himself in love with Mary.

But the timid and submissive Fanny resists all pressures, even
makes her own modest statement of women's rights. It is surely
minimal – "I think it ought not to be set down as certain that a man
must be acceptable to every woman he may happen to like himself" – yet more daring than it seems, given her natural timidity and
her dependent position. It is of course ignored. The one reason that
might satisfy Sir Thomas, Fanny's deep disapproval of Crawford's behavior and character, based on his flirtations with Julia and Maria,
she cannot give because it would shame the Bertram daughters.

Fanny, then, must hold out against both the strong disapproval
of a guardian whom she holds in awe and the courtship of a suitor
who is a wit and a man of fashion, who is able to please everyone
except herself. It might seem that she succeeds too easily, that she
resists temptation because she is never tempted. Her recurring won-
der as to whether Henry really has changed – on seeing him at
Portsmouth, "She thought him altogether improved . . . much more
gentle, obliging, and attentive to other people's feelings" – implies
no beginning of love. Even granting the possibility of his "turning out
well at last," he nonetheless "was and must ever be completely un-
suited to her," as most readers would surely agree.

The true test for Fanny is not in refusing this offer of a brilliant
marriage but in daring to assert her moral independence by rejecting
the awesome authority of Sir Thomas. What Crawford can offer,
whether himself or his rank and fortune and estate, does not tempt
her. His prolonged courtship, his intervention with Sir Thomas, his
repeated efforts, aided by his sister, to put Fanny in his debt – even
to the extent of using his influence to secure a promotion in the navy
for her brother, William – all fail. But given her timidity, her dependent position, and the urgings of Edmund and her respect and gratitude toward Sir Thomas (a more powerful influence than any desire
for rank or wealth could be) – her steady rejection of Crawford's
suit appears almost heroic.

Readers have found Crawford's attraction to such a woman, even as
a source of temporary amusement, unrealistic and out of character.
Yet the explanation the text supplies, beyond his need for continuous diversion, is a powerful one – his male egotism: on seeing

Fanny's devotion to her brother, William, he realizes that "It would be something to be loved by such a girl, to excite the first ardours of her young unsophisticated mind!" And he has, if not morality, then at least sufficient "moral taste" (a subtle distinction) to recognize the beauty of such a devotion.

Ironically, it is Crawford who is caught. "She interested him more than he had foreseen," and that interest increases. But his tactics are still those of the hunter. He aims to trap his victim by forcing her into a sense of obligation – most effectively, by getting William's promotion. But trickery is used as well, with his sister's connivance. The necklace Fanny reluctantly agrees to wear at her coming-out ball because she believes it to be Mary's turns out to be in effect a gift from Henry. Mary Crawford, who had deceived her, proves "careless as a woman and a friend." Loyalty, whether of man to woman, sister to sister, or woman to woman, is a major virtue in this novel, even though presented mainly through its violation. But Crawford's appreciation of Fanny, while increasing the complexity and interest of his character, is revealing in its limitations. It is patronizing – she is his "little Fanny" – and his devotion is carefully qualified by Mary's prediction that "even when you ceased to love, she would yet find in you the liberality and good breeding of a gentleman."

Parallel to Crawford's courtship of Fanny runs Mary's pursuit of Edmund. The basic situation is the same – the attraction of the sophisticated outsider, the townsman or woman, to the simplicity and moral directness of Mansfield Park. And Mary, like Henry, desires not simply love, but conquest. She is delighted by recalling Edmund's surrender of principle in taking a part during the rehearsals of *Lovers' Vows:* "I never knew such exquisite happiness . . . His sturdy spirit to bend as it did! It was sweet beyond expression."

Mansfield Park itself, with the old-fashioned virtues for which it stands – respect for the family, for tradition, for authority, for social responsibility (note Henry's neglect of his own estate), for religion as represented by the established church – all seem about to be subverted by the Crawfords. Its survival depends on Fanny, not on Edmund, who has more than half capitulated – and Fanny is compelled to resist pressure from all those around her, even from her uncle. Sir Thomas is completely taken in by the Crawfords and – just as with Maria's engagement to Rushworth – seems blinded to clear incompatibility by the worldly advantages of such a marriage. As Fanny

comes to understand, "delicacy," in the Austenian sense, is not to be
expected from a man who had married his daughter to a Rushworth.
Lady Bertram's opinion, in the only piece of advice she ever gives her
niece, is exactly the same: "it is every young woman's duty to accept
such a very unexceptionable offer as this." Of course Fanny resists,
passing all tests of character – perhaps too easily. Fanny will be required to withstand intense pressure from those she respects most,
but there is never any doubt in her own mind as to rightness of her
decision.

Some of Austen's contemporary readers apparently felt uncertain
till the last as to whether Fanny would, or should, finally accept
Crawford. Even her brother James, while reading *Mansfield Park*,
"defied anybody to say" whether Crawford "would be reformed, or
would forget Fanny in a fortnight." Clearly, James was no critic. A
true "reformation" by Henry Crawford, leading no doubt to his final
acceptance by Fanny, would have destroyed the moral scheme of the
novel, replacing it with the tritest of "happy endings" – the rake reformed by the influence of a good woman – and nullified its social
implications as well. *Mansfield Park* would have become merely a
conventional romance.

Yet Austen herself momentarily encourages readers to believe
that such an ending might have been possible, commenting (after
Henry's elopement with Maria) that "Could he have been satisfied
with the conquest of one amiable woman's affections. . . . Would he
have persevered, and uprightly, Fanny must have been his reward."
If only he had "done as he intended, and as he knew he ought" – by
going straight to his estate of Everingham after leaving
Portsmouth – "he might have been deciding his own happy des-
tiny." But the barrier between them, as Fanny recognizes, is psychological as well as moral. They seem hopelessly incompatible. In
any case, a character who could, convincingly, have avoided the
temptations of the town and of Maria would not have been the
Henry Crawford we have seen for some 400 pages.

The adulterous affair between Henry and Maria does not seem
improbable in itself. That he should delay the visit to his estate to dip
into the pleasures of London society, that he should meet Maria and
be challenged by her indifference, that he should work to overcome
that indifference and that she should respond, that flirtation should
lead to adultery and discovery – and all this without Crawford's ever

intending actual seduction, much less elopement, or even being unfaithful in his own mind to Fanny – all this seems entirely consistent with the impression of him, and of Maria as well, that the novel has created.

The difficulty for modern readers in accepting this outcome is essentially moral – the impossibility of accepting the double standard that exiles Maria from society forever, while Crawford – who had made the first advance – goes unpunished except for losing any hope of winning Fanny. That outcome may seem inevitable, given the time and place and circumstances, but it cannot seem justified. Modern readers are likely to take Mary Crawford's view, which rouses Edmund's indignation – "She saw it only as folly," rather than as criminal. Sir Thomas's refusal to sanction vice by bringing Maria into his home inevitably recalls Mr. Collins's advice to Mr. Bennet "to forgive them [Lydia and Wickham] as a Christian, but never admit them to your sight, or allow their names to be mentioned in your hearing." "And that is his idea of Christian forgiveness!" exclaims Mr. Bennet.

It is apparently Sir Thomas's idea also, and the moral and religious authority he should embody, in spite of his errors, is correspondingly weakened. Christian charity and recognition that all men and women are sinners do not seem to be part of the religion of Mansfield. In fact, for all of Fanny's piety, *Mansfield Park* can be considered a Christian novel only in a limited sense. Its emphasis is not on religious belief in itself, as a transcendental value, but rather on its importance as a necessary support of the established moral code, seen as essential both to a meaningful personal life and an ordered society.

Wit itself becomes suspect – surprising as that might seem in a novel by the author of *Pride and Prejudice*. But here, wit is unreliable, probably subversive. The Crawfords' liveliness, perhaps their most valuable quality, comes under suspicion as well. It is misdirected and therefore subversive. Maria, we are told, had encountered Crawford while visiting "a family of lively, agreeable manners, and probably of morals and discretion to suit." "Lively and agreeable manners" – a phrase that would exactly describe the manners of Elizabeth Bennet – are made synonymous with sexual looseness. It almost goes without saying that Fanny, Edmund, and Sir Thomas are all without the least capacity for irony. As Trilling observes, "one might almost say that it [*Mansfield Park*] undertakes to discredit irony and to affirm literalness," to demonstrate "that there are no two ways about anything" (Trilling, 125). Not that irony is entirely excluded – unthinkable, in an Austen novel – but that is reserved for the narrative voice and is exercised largely at the expense of the antihero and antiheroine. Sir Thomas, in particular, seems to be let off very lightly.

All of which is not to say that *Mansfield Park* is a failure – rather, that it is a brilliant, flawed novel, and flawed principally in its conclusion. "Let other pens dwell on guilt and misery," reads the opening sentence of the final chapter, and the author's repugnance – even loathing – for what she narrates is unmistakable. It is not primarily the ending itself, the actual events presented, that arouses objection, but the satisfaction with which they are narrated and punishment is inflicted, at least on Maria. Commonly, in reading fiction, we become aware of ideology only when it forces itself on our attention – when at some critical point, as in the elopement of Crawford and Maria and the punishment inflicted on Maria, we are clearly expected to respond in a way that has become impossible.

But the implications of *Mansfield Park* are not necessarily confined by the morality of its own time, which can seem so harsh and restrictive. What Mansfield stands for – an existence based on order and principle in contrast to the light modernity and selfish pleasure seeking of the Crawfords – deserves respect, if not affection.

Chapter Six

Emma

"My greatest anxiety at present," wrote Austen just before the publication of *Emma*, "is that this fourth work should not disgrace what was good in the others." She was "very strongly haunted with the idea that to those readers who have preferred 'Pride and Prejudice' it will appear inferior in wit, and to those who have preferred 'Mansfield Park' very inferior in good sense" (*Letters*, 443). To judge by the opinions of *Emma* that she collected, Austen's anxiety seems to have been well-founded. Opinions ranged from the implicit approval of "Mr. Jeffrey" (Francis Jeffrey, one of the most influential critics of the day), who "was kept up by it three nights" (*Memoir*, 97), to the total condemnation of a Miss Murden, who thought it "certainly inferior to all the others."[1] Readers preferred *Pride and Prejudice* for its wit, *Mansfield Park* for its morality. They admired *Emma*'s Mr. Knightley, but they could not admire Emma.

It is only in the twentieth century that the unique qualities of *Emma* have been recognized. Recognized among critics, that is, for *Pride and Prejudice* remains the public's favorite. Self-confident, often domineering – and therefore "masculine" by traditional stereotyping – Emma Woodhouse is not a lovable heroine. (What other heroine of the eighteenth- or nineteenth-century English novel would declare, "I always deserve the best treatment, because I never put up with any other"?[2] Vain, egotistical, overbearing, Emma seems almost too flawed to be a proper heroine. As if realizing this, she tries instead to create a heroine of her own, Harriet.

But claims can be made for *Emma*. It is very nearly a flawless novel – the most carefully constructed of Austen's works – and it is the purest comedy of them all. (Not that emotion is lacking; comedy without feeling soon wearies the reader.) Technically, it is masterful in Austen's control of point of view and of information, deceiving the reader along with the heroine. In this respect, *Emma* is surely one of the most original novels of its century – a surprising claim, perhaps, since Austen has certainly not been generally credited with such originality. But such a novel, in which readers are required to share the heroine's limited knowledge and consequently to share also in her blunders and surprises, was unprecedented, creating a unique psychological realism and, incidentally, creating a necessary feeling of charity toward Emma and her errors.

Criticism may begin with an obvious question: what is *Emma* about? Simple formulas will not do – *Emma* is about self-discovery, or the discrepancy between appearance and reality, or even human fallibility. Any novel worth discussing can be shown to deal with at least one of these themes, and probably with them all. What "happens" in *Emma* is far too complex to be contained in such an easy summary. Simple statements of "theme," abstracted from the realities of the work, are useless. A more adequate answer might be that *Emma* is about the process by which Emma Woodhouse, motivated by love of power and pride in her own intellectual and social superiority, meddles arrogantly and ignorantly in the affairs of various people both in her circle and out of it, at the risk of their happiness and ultimately her own, until a series of humiliations reveals her as mistaken about the feelings not only of her neighbors but of herself. Since the tone is comic, she cannot be allowed to do any really serious or permanent damage, although she must cause enough pain to justify her final remorse and shame. Finally, Emma achieves a self-insight that makes possible her union with Mr. Knightley. As Julia Brown puts it, at the center of *Emma*, as of every Austen novel, "stands that archetypal figure, the uncommitted young woman."[3] Of all Austen's heroines, it is Emma who seeks commitment most energetically, although often with comically disastrous results.

Taking this or some similar statement not merely as "theme" but as a basic organizing principle, almost every detail can be seen to follow from it. It dictates the method by which the story should be told – almost entirely from Emma's point of view. (There is only one significant exception. In chapter 5 of volume 3, readers look through Knightley's eyes and share his responses, as he watches Frank Churchill playing his game with the box of wooden letters – amusing himself at the expense of both Jane and Emma – and gives his disregarded warning to Emma: "Do you think you perfectly understand the degree of understanding?" between Frank and Jane.) *Emma* is the longest of Austen's novels. It is also the most concentrated, the most tightly unified – an effect resulting directly from this focus on Emma's point of view.

Such a central principle will determine not only what must be included but what is to be left out. Some readers have found the characterization of Jane Fairfax a failure: "cold, pale Jane" is Reginald Farrer's summary (Farrer, 2:269). Others have felt that they would have liked to see more and know more of Jane Fairfax. But what would readers think of Emma, the heroine, if they saw her from Jane's point of view? Emma may be guilty of unpardonable arrogance, but nevertheless readers must pardon her. And in any case, to have given more prominence to Jane would have destroyed the balance of the novel – her problems are so much greater than Emma's, the possible outcome for her so much more serious. Jane's position is so desperate, her suffering and her suspense must be so keen, that if readers were once taken inside her consciousness, she would promptly displace Emma as the center of interest and a radically different novel would result. There would be little place for comedy in such a story, and there would also be little action – Jane, unlike Emma, is almost entirely helpless. The only thing she can do, other than to suffer and to wait, is to break her engagement to Frank Churchill.

Only once, late in the novel, is she allowed an outcry that partly reveals the misery of her situation: "Oh! Miss Woodhouse, the comfort of being sometimes alone." Certainly the presence of both Jane and Miss Bates in the same novel strongly supports Alistair Duckworth's remark that "the predicament of the unsupported woman was never far from Jane Austen's thoughts."[4] Still, in this novel Emma remains the center of interest, with all other characters seen through her eyes.

Again, as in *Sense and Sensibility* and *Pride and Prejudice*, Austen presents sharply contrasting heroines. Jane and Emma are the same age, and both are beautiful and intelligent, but in their personalities, their situations, and their prospects they seem exactly opposite. Jane is "very elegant, remarkably elegant," and Emma is not – she has too much energy for elegance, even though she admires it. "Elegance," in fact, while admired, is surprisingly rare in Austen's novels; of her primary heroines, only Anne Elliot possesses it. Mrs. Elton is only a pretender, no more truly elegant than she is truly sophisticated. She has, as Emma soon suspects, "ease but not elegance." She may declare that she admires Mr. Woodhouse's "quaint, old-fashioned politeness," that it is much more to her taste than "modern ease," but in fact she is the embodiment of "modern ease." Her speeches define the term.

Wealthy and secure in her status, Emma is about to enter adult life, while Jane – to all appearances at least – is preparing "to retire from all the pleasures of life, of rational intercourse, equal society, peace and hope, to penance and mortification for ever" – to become a governess, in short. The language is so strong that it's hard to avoid wondering whether Austen herself, as an educated single woman, without money, had ever dreaded that fate. But Jane's situation does not allow her to become prominent – she can only wait for some lucky accident to save her. In fact, two such accidents are required: first, that Frank Churchill should fall in love with Jane and engage himself to her, in spite of his fear of his domineering foster mother, Mrs. Churchill, and second, that Mrs. Churchill should die before she can compel Frank to choose between love and his expectations as the Churchill's heir.

Readers of *Emma* – first-time readers, that is – participate in the action as they try to make sense of the situation together with the heroine, sharing her knowledge, her insights, and her errors, and so comprehending her humiliation as she learns the truth. But solving the mystery of Jane Fairfax's presence in Highbury in no way reduces the pleasure that *Emma* offers in rereading. All of Austen's novels are rich in detail and eminently reward rereading, but to return to *Pride and Prejudice*, after a reasonable interval, is to experience pleasure similar to that of a first reading, perhaps heightened by anticipation of some favorite scene or passage. *Emma*, too, provides that sort of pleasure, as we look forward to the heroine's succession of comic blunders and embarrassments and to the satisfaction of seeing such overweening conceit and self-confidence thoroughly put down. It is only human to want Emma to be mistaken and to know it and to suffer deep embarrassment.

But rereading *Emma* offers another reward, impossible on first reading – the innumerable ironies to be enjoyed as one recognizes the discrepancies between Emma's view of things and the actual situation. *Emma* becomes, in effect, a different novel and for many readers an even more interesting one. Farrer has seriously proposed that *Emma* "should never be published without a prefatory synopsis" because the experience of rereading is "richer and more satisfying . . . than a first reading can possibly be" (Farrer, 2:266).

With her usual clarity and economy, Austen outlines the essential qualities of her protagonist in the opening sentence: "Emma Woodhouse, handsome, clever, and rich, with a comfortable and happy disposition, seemed to unite some of the best blessings of existence; and had lived nearly twenty-one years in the world with very little to distress or vex her." That sentence guarantees not only that this rare immunity of the heroine from distress and vexation is about to end but also that *Emma* is to be a very different book from its predecessor. Forceful, decisive, self-confident, in her personality and her situation, Emma is as different from Fanny Price as Fanny is from Elizabeth Bennet. With her energy and intelligence, Emma may seem to resemble Elizabeth. But while intelligent, she lacks Elizabeth's sharp wit, and in her meddlesomeness and love of directing other people's lives can at times appear to resemble Lady Catherine de Bourgh instead.

But there is a more important difference between these two heroines. Elizabeth can be mistaken, as in her initial misjudgment of Wickham, or in her decision that it's better not to reveal his true character, but Emma's mistakes are of an entirely different kind. She is an "imaginist" – a word probably of Austen's own invention – constantly distorting reality to fit her own schemes and preconceptions. In a sense, she is a novelist herself, although her plots seem hackneyed – marrying Harriet above her station, whether with Mr. Elton or with Frank Churchill, imagining Jane Fairfax involved in an intrigue with the unseen Mr. Dixon, the husband of her foster-sister, Miss Campbell – that "ingenious and animating suspicion," as the narrator ironically calls it, which is encouraged by Frank Churchill.

Emma's situation – in effect the only daughter of a wealthy but helpless father who entirely depends on her, allowing her to control his household and his fortune – is radically different from that of any other Austen heroine. It simultaneously encourages and partly excuses her domineering ways and her interference in other people's affairs. As Knightley observes to Mrs. Weston, Emma's former governess, "She has been mistress of the house and of you all" since she was 12 years old. It would be easy to imagine Emma developing into an officious, meddling "great lady." In fact, her consuming egotism might make her more dangerous to those in her power than the open tyranny of a Lady Catherine or a Mrs. Ferrars. Harriet at times is very nearly turned into a ventriloquist's dummy; on reading Mr. Elton's charade, she "was all flutter and happiness. She could not speak. But she was not wanted to speak. Emma spoke for her."

Emma's good looks were no doubt required by literary convention. Even Fanny Price, in *Mansfield Park*, seems to grow more beautiful, or at least prettier, as she becomes a principal actor rather than merely an observer. But Emma's kind of beauty is relevant to her character. She is "handsome," a word implying a decisive, "masculine" quality (and Emma is the only Austen heroine so described). Not only does she rule her household, but wealth and family background give her unquestioned supremacy in Highbury – a kind of supremacy that no other Austen heroine enjoys. Her security must be shaken or destroyed (or there could be no novel), and consequently – barring melodramatic disasters of a kind that as a rule do not occur in Austen's novels – readers can expect that any threats to the happiness of a heroine so advantaged are likely to result from her own mistakes. And in fact Emma is the most active of Austen's heroines, although in most cases her activity is misguided, futile, and self-defeating, because based on her misunderstanding of the actual situation – that Mr. Elton is courting Harriet rather than herself, that Jane is in love with the unseen Mr. Dixon, that Harriet loves Frank Churchill for rescuing her from gypsies, when in fact she has fallen in love with Knightley when he danced with her after Mr. Elton's snub.

The character of Emma poses a difficult problem – one that could have been avoided had Austen decided to take the easy course of treating her satirically, showing her up as the meddlesome snob that she so often appears to be. But Emma is not the butt of a satire, and readers must be enabled to preserve a difficult balance between sympathy and detachment and should relish her well-deserved suffering and self-condemnation – her behavior can be outrageous – while wishing for her final happiness. There are those who find that balance impossible, who cannot tolerate the mixture of snobbery and egotism that for them makes up the character of Emma. Austen feared that she had created a heroine whom nobody would like but herself, and the reception of *Emma* throughout the nineteenth century almost seemed to prove that she was right.

There is no danger of anyone's admiring Emma uncritically, as there certainly can be in the case of Elizabeth Bennet, or taking her for a model of Christian virtues, as Fanny Price at times appears to be. The danger, with Emma, is in the opposite direction, and the author employs a wide variety of techniques to avoid excessive hostility toward the heroine. Most important is the point of view itself, forcing readers to share many of her blunders and therefore not condemn her too harshly. There are extenuating circumstances as well. Emma is domineering, but dominance is forced upon her by the early death of her mother and by her father's abdication of all responsibility, by the weakness of her governess, and of course by her own intelligence and strength of will. In the spirit of comedy, *Emma* is far more forgiving than *Mansfield Park* – not only to its flawed heroine but to Frank Churchill (in spite of his frivolity and his cruelty to Jane), to Jane herself (for entering into a secret engagement – "What has it been but a system of hypocrisy and deceit, – espionage and treachery?" in Emma's words), and even to the spiteful, officious Eltons (whose only punishment is simply to go on being themselves).

The novel ultimately demonstrates that Emma really is superior – in manners, intelligence, taste, force of character – to everyone in Highbury except Knightley and perhaps Jane Fairfax. Even her snobbery is presented as the excess of a virtue – her genuine passion for the first-rate. Her avoidance of Miss Bates is uncharitable, but it grows out of a "horror of being in danger of falling in with the second and third rate of Highbury." And such fastidiousness seems more acceptable when contrasted with the indiscriminate heartiness of a Weston. Amiable and well-meaning as Weston is, readers gradually lose respect for him as they see him giving away secrets and mixing incompatible people, until with Emma herself they realize the drawbacks of "such unmanageable good will." Similarly, the harsh unsociability of John Knightley represents an opposite extreme, with his brother occupying the desirable mean.

Emma is set off to her own advantage to a still greater degree by Mrs. Elton, a parody of the heroine who exaggerates all her faults and diverts to herself the dislike that might otherwise be felt toward Emma. She shares Emma's need to dominate and to be admired. Her manners are worse, her meddling and interference in other people's affairs more open, her egotism cruder and more offensive, but the really significant difference between the two is Emma's greater intelligence. It is this intelligence that allows her to understand the consequences of her actions and to learn from her mistakes, as Mrs. Elton never does. Instead, her vicious snobbery, her vanity, her rudeness and impertinent familiarity masquerading as "sparkling vivacity," all contrive to make Emma's similar failings appear less serious in comparison and her genuine accomplishments and qualities to seem all the more valuable. Mrs. Elton's hostility to Emma is important as well – condemnation from her is praise, and increases sympathy for the heroine.

Basic to the characterization of Mrs. Elton is her need to be admired – another quality she shares with Emma. This compulsion takes obvious forms – dressing showily, boasting about the wealth of her connections in Bristol and the number of her own servants (so many, it appears, that she can't be expected to remember their names) – but also manifests itself more surprisingly and more interestingly. Her obsession with current fads, her desperate desire to appear up to date and sophisticated – to ride a donkey if that's what ladies do in the countryside, to refer to her husband as her "caro sposo," her "lord and master," or "Mr. E." – combine to make her seem a curiously modern figure while also showing her total lack of self-knowledge. Never does Mrs. Elton seem more like a parody of Emma than when she remarks, "I had no fear of retirement. Blessed with so many resources within myself, the world was not necessary to *me*. I could do very well without it." Inevitably, readers recall Emma's forecast of her future life – "If I draw less, I shall read more; if I give up music, I shall take up carpet-work." Mrs. Elton's "apparatus of happiness" is a striking, almost paradoxical phrase – what does happiness have to do with "apparatus"? – and that confusion, too, seems typically modern. Yet Mrs. Elton is no hypocrite, that traditional target of satire, but a more complex and interesting figure. Before deceiving, or attempting to deceive, others, she deceives herself as to the sort of person she is.

Harriet Smith, "the natural daughter of somebody," with her docility, her empty mind, her youth – she is 17 to Emma's almost 21 – and her social inferiority offers an irresistible temptation to Emma's love of power. (Mrs. Elton, by contrast, in making herself the patron of Jane, chooses a protegé who is much more intelligent than herself – a fact which of course she does not recognize.) Ironically, it is just this vagueness, this apparently infinite malleability, that protects Harriet and saves Emma. It might seem that by persuading her to reject Mr. Martin's proposal, Emma has destroyed Harriet's best chance for happiness – certainly in doing so has displayed her own snobbery at its worst in her assumption that a farmer *must* belong to "the society of the illiterate and vulgar."

But readers are never allowed to become greatly concerned about Harriet – there are no inside views of her thoughts and feelings – or to forget the "many vacancies" of her mind. And the novel has demonstrated that she is capable of falling in or out of love in a moment. *Emma* is a comedy, and comedies traditionally end with marriages. It is clear that Harriet will marry Robert Martin in the end – and Emma's realization that "It would be a great pleasure to know Robert Martin" indicates the depth and genuineness of her own change. But for Harriet to lose Martin would not be tragic. He is no doubt the best husband she is likely to find, but readers know that, as Knightley observes, she is the kind of girl who will certainly marry somebody or other. Probably the best evidence that Harriet may finally have learned something, whether from association with Emma or simply from growing up, can be found in her preferring Knightley to Frank Churchill.

A novel, in the convention that Austen accepted, requires a hero. Knightley fills that role in a deeper sense than by merely providing a husband for the heroine at the conclusion. One measure of his importance is the simple fact that unlike any other Austen hero, even Edmund Bertram, he is present from beginning to end. Throughout *Emma* he acts as commentator, largely though not entirely replacing the author. The choice of his name, both realistic and appropriate, is daring yet successful. He is indeed "knightly," in all ways appropriate to a peaceful society, yet no character could seem less like an allegorical figure. He is the most important and the most fully characterized of Austen's heroes, made "real" through the force of his language – terse, objective, rational (though not unemotional), contrasting particularly with the ambiguous, often nonsensical compliments of Mr. Elton when he is courting Emma – through his constant presence, and through his relationships with every other character.

He is by far the most mature of the heroes – and not only in age. Of them all, he has the least to learn (but the one thing he must learn is crucial – that he loves Emma). At any point, he can simultaneously tell both Emma and the reader precisely how she is mistaken, and since his comments are so obviously sound, most readers quickly learn to accept his judgment in any difference with other characters. For some readers, of course, Knightley is too nearly perfect, or too positive (and always right as well), too authoritative, too much a representative of established (male) authority. But Austen's novels do not express antagonism toward authority simply because it is established.

As his name implies, Knightley embodies the major virtues of this novel, and all of Austen's novels. (Although he is given very human weaknesses, such as his unacknowledged jealousy of Frank Churchill and his rationalization of his own motives for revealing his suspicions of Churchill to Emma – that he must "as a friend – an anxious friend – give Emma some hint" of his suspicions.) The entire characterization of Knightley implies that the virtues he embodies are attainable by ordinary human beings living in society. Emma's final union with him represents her acceptance, and adoption, of those values – particularly of openness. "Mr. Knightley does nothing mysteriously," as Mrs. Weston observes, while Emma's schemes constantly lead her into what Knightley calls "maneuvres" and "finesse." That alone would condemn them, even without their disastrous results. Absolute candor may be impossible – "Seldom, very seldom, does complete truth belong to any human disclosure," Austen observes with her usual sense of human limitations – but it's in large part from Knightley that Emma learns the value of even such incomplete truth as can be communicated. Finally, only a hero like Knightley could persuade readers that the ending is truly happy. Emma requires a husband who is her equal, in both intellect and strength of will.

Knightley's character can also be considered as in a sense "timely." *Emma*, like all novels, is the product of a particular moment in history. Composed 20 years earlier or later, it would necessarily have been a different book. As it is, written near the end of England's long war with France – a war in which national survival had often seemed at stake – *Emma* necessarily reflects that sense of struggle. Not in the actual lives of its characters, which hardly seem to be affected at all (much less so than in *Mansfield Park* or *Persuasion*), or through ideological statements, but rather in the intense "Englishness" of Highbury, its inhabitants and its countryside. *Emma* seems a microcosm of England such as appears nowhere else in Austen's work. That quality of "Englishness," as Austen perceived it, becomes explicit during the strawberry picking at Donwell Abbey. The description of the house itself – "rambling and irregular, with many comfortable and one or two handsome rooms" – can easily be read as symbolic of Austen's England and its society, an organic growth, over centuries, as contrasted with such artificial creations as the French Republic and Napoleon's Empire. The name itself, "Donwell Abbey," creates a sense of history, and ideology becomes unmistakable in the description of the view from the Abbey grounds – the Abbey-Mill farm, with its meadows and orchards, backed by a curving river and a steep, wooded bank – and above all in the summing up: "It was a sweet view – sweet to the eye and the mind. English verdure, English culture, English comfort, seen under a sun bright, without being oppressive." This is an England in miniature, an ideal England.

Knightley, in turn, can be seen as the ideal Englishman, notably in his detestation of secrecy. Everything he does is done openly, and this is a virtue that Emma must learn from him. Frank Churchill, his opposite, continually practices "maneuvres" and "finesse." "So unlike what a man should be!" is Emma's final judgment on him. The qualities that are lacking in Frank – the "upright integrity," the "strict adherence to truth and principle," and particularly the "disdain of trick and littleness" that "a man should display in every transaction of his life" – these qualities are continually exhibited by Knightley. It is Emma's recognition of their true value that marks her reformation and her realization that Knightley is the man she must marry.

Knightley is energetic in everything he does ("He staid on, vigorously," we are told, when visiting his brother in London). It is a quality he shares with Emma, although his energy is used constructively. He is presented as thoroughly masculine – strong, hardy (he is out of doors in all weathers), decisive, open – yet he is no stereotypically plain, blunt Englishman. For instance, Frank Churchill is, as Knightley says, "amiable" only in French. He is "*aimable*" – the

French term meaning "to have very good manners and be very agreeable," but he lacks the "delicacy towards the feelings of other people" signified by the English "amiable." This amiability, or "delicacy," is a quality Knightley is shown to possess to a greater degree than any other character in *Emma*, including its heroine. It is most conspicuously displayed during the ball at the Crown, when Knightley recognizes Harriet's embarrassment and humiliation, after Mr. Elton's public rejection of her as a partner, and dances with her himself. Again, Austen resists sexual stereotyping; such sensitivity has traditionally been considered a female quality, but Knightley possesses it just as Emma possesses an energy and decisiveness often attributed to men.

As well as a hero and a heroine, an Austen novel requires its fools and bores. Mr. Woodhouse and Miss Bates play those roles in *Emma*. (Both Eltons certainly talk and behave foolishly enough at times, but they are significantly more complex figures – as a comparison of Mr. Elton with Mr. Collins instantly reveals.) Modern readers are likely to feel impatient with Mr. Woodhouse, a wealthy hypochondriac who is utterly useless to society. The Victorian critic A. C. Bradley's judgment that Mr. Woodhouse is, next to Don Quixote, the most perfect gentleman in fiction, seems to come from a world more distant than Austen's.[5] He is Emma's "paternal jailor," he "battens on Emma, thwarting her own healthy instinct for living," observes one critic.[6] But in the novel itself, he is "the kind-hearted, polite old man," and those qualities seem to make up for all his deficiencies.

While his limitations – "his talents could not have recommended him at any time" – and his "gentle selfishness" are clearly stated and shown, the easy opening for devastating satire is passed by. The friendliness of Mr. Woodhouse's heart and his amiable temper make amends for everything with his Highbury neighbors, and for much with the author. He cannot advance the action, yet he is an essential part of Emma's environment. His helplessness explains and excuses her managing ways, and her treatment of him displays a tenderness and a steadiness in performing a duty, often very dull, that works to prevent readers from judging her too harshly. Like Miss Bates, he serves as a moral touchstone, revealing the characters of others by their attitudes toward him. Knightley seems destined to become Emma's husband for many reasons, but one of the most important is his affectionate tolerance of her father.

Like Mr. Woodhouse, Miss Bates cannot act, but contributes immeasurably to the reader's sense of Highbury as a living community – to a degree that is unique in Austen's novels, with its gentlemen and its half-gentlemen, its school for girls, its shopkeepers and its physician and its neighboring farmers, although these are referred to rather than seen). She is the recognized town gossip, its gatherer and dispenser of news. It is surely a critical error to assume that "the attentions heaped upon her are painfully patronizing." Her role in unifying, or binding together, her community is essential – at times it seems as if most of the population of Highbury is gathered in her little apartment or passing by on the street, underneath her window – and in a sense her service is recognized and paid for, since she and her mother are partly supported by the charity of their neighbors.

Emma's treatment of Miss Bates, then, is not only uncharitable and snobbish but unsociable as well – at times she appears to believe that a Miss Woodhouse ought not to take interest in mere local gossip. But Miss Bates's monologues are considerably more than that. They are highly comic in themselves, and they contribute importantly toward creating a sense of Highbury as a community, which is unique in Austen's novels. They also frequently reveal significant information concerning the relationship between Jane Fairfax and Frank Churchill, information that might have enabled Emma to guess the truth – so sparing herself much embarrassment – but that she stubbornly misinterprets, preferring her own, almost slanderous misinterpretation of Jane's presence, that she is in love with the unseen Mr. Dixon, and even that she may be in correspondence with him. (One of the pleasures of rereading *Emma* is to recognize these moments when the heroine is totally mistaken, just when she is proudest of her insight.)

But Miss Bates differs from Austen's other fools. She is laughable, yet with her total unselfishness and benevolence, her readiness to see only the best in everyone, her forgiveness of insult, combined with her poverty (of which she seems almost unaware) she is as close to sainthood as Highbury can come. Her monologues are essential to the story, but her single most important function may be to receive Emma's insult at Box Hill. She is good, she is dull, she is de-

fenseless – these qualities that provoke the attack also make it inexcusable. She is touchingly, yet irresistibly, vulnerable: "I shall be sure
to say three dull things as soon as ever I open my mouth, shan't I?"
When Emma strikes – "Ah! Ma'am, but there may be a difficulty.
Pardon me – but you will be limited to number – only three at
once" – readers are likely to share the exhilaration of this plain
speaking, this throwing off the mask of civility to reveal Miss Bates at
last as the bore that she is. Yet this is the worst thing Emma has
done, and to approve, even for a moment, is to become her accom-
plice and consequently to feel the force of Knightley's rebuke: "How
could you be so unfeeling. . . . How could you be so insolent in your
wit to a woman of her character, age and situation?"

The consequence, for Emma, is remarkable – those "extra- ordinary" tears that she feels "running down her cheeks almost all the
way home." Emma has not only felt guilt, but for the first time in the
novel she has realized the importance to her of Knightley's opinion.
Penance is immediate, with the visit of expiation to Miss Bates the
next day, a visit made all the more painful by Miss Bates's "dreadful
gratitude" – a striking phrase against the background of Austen's
carefully restrained language. The immediate result of that scene is
Knightley's reaction when he learns of it: "He took her hand,
pressed it, and was certainly on the point of carrying it to his
lips – when, from some fancy or other, he suddenly let it go." Manners are highly decorous in Austen's novels, with outward expres-
sions of emotion a rarity. Knightley's gesture, then, is moving, both
for readers and for Emma. Emma misinterprets that gesture, as she
misinterprets so much else – "It spoke such perfect amity." But
readers know better. It spoke love, not amity.

The union of heroine and hero must not come about so easily,
or so soon. The secret engagement must be revealed – and the more
that readers learn of Frank Churchill's behavior, the higher Mr.
Knightley's stands in comparison. Next, Emma's pride in her own
discernment receives its greatest shock, with Harriet's revelation that
she is in love with Knightley rather than Frank (as Emma had believed). In three remarkable pages of remorseless self-analysis,
unique in Austen's novels, the heroine is made to accept entire responsibility for the situation and to confess that she has misunderstood everything, "had been imposed on by others in a most mortifying degree . . . had been imposing on herself in a degree yet more

mortifying; that she was wretched and should probably find this day but the beginning of wretchedness." (The greatest difference between Emma Woodhouse and Elizabeth Bennet is not that Emma is less witty, but that she is self-conscious and self-analytical.) The situation is unparalleled in Austen's work – only when the novel is more than four-fifths completed does the heroine realize that she is in love with the hero.

Emma's inner response to Harriet's declaration is certainly the most sudden and dramatic realization of love in Austen's novels: "It darted through her, with the speed of an arrow, that Mr. Knightley must marry no one but herself!" The proposal scene follows inevitably, yet is unexpected by the heroine and unintended by the hero – a comedy of misunderstandings, with Knightley believing that Emma is in love with Frank Churchill and is grieving at the news of his engagement to Jane Fairfax, and Emma convinced that Knightley is about to reveal his love for Harriet and consequently discouraging him from speaking, when in fact he is longing to say what she most wishes to hear – to declare his love for her. And once again Emma is proved wrong, this time misunderstanding herself as much as she has misunderstood others – to be in love, she had thought, "is not my way or my nature." In the context of the novel, this is no concession to social pressures but a recognition of her own human needs and desires. As for her conventional response to Knightley's passionate declaration – "What did she say? – Just what she ought, of course. A lady always does." – it certainly should not be taken as evidence of Austen's embarrassment or discomfort in handling deep feeling, but in fact is entirely appropriate to the situation. In her surprise and confusion, in the chaotic state of her feelings, when she has abruptly moved from despair to the realization that what she most wants and needs is now hers, Emma's one resource is to fall back on conventionalities.

Critics have doubted that Emma actually "reforms" herself – Austen "does not ask us to concern ourselves beyond the happy ending: she merely presents the evidence, noncommittally," writes Mudrick (196) – but this seems a clear misreading. There is Emma's own declaration to Jane Fairfax: "Oh! if you knew how much I love everything that is decided and open!" And even if we distrust that statement, we can be convinced that change is real, that the happy ending is truly happy, by the final paragraph, contrasting Mrs.

Elton's opinion of the wedding – "Very little white satin, very few lace veils; a most pitiful business!" – with the author's assurance that "in spite of these deficiencies, the wishes, the hopes, the confidence, the predictions of the small band of true friends who witnessed the ceremony, were fully answered in the perfect happiness of the union." Readers who remain skeptical as to the future happiness of both Emma and Knightley will find themselves in the uncomfortable position of agreeing with Mrs. Elton.

Chapter Seven

Persuasion

In *Persuasion*, many readers have seen indications that Austen's work, if she had lived, might have developed in strikingly new directions. Certainly its inwardness, its subjectivity, it concentration from beginning to end on the emotions of Anne Elliot – its focused interiority, one might say – is unprecedented in her work, as is the depth of passion that makes the final reconciliation between Anne Elliot and Captain Wentworth one of the most moving love scenes in the English novel. Yet this sustained intensity of feeling is combined with both a satirical harshness, notably in the presentation of Sir Walter Elliot, the heroine's father, that is unmatched in Austen's earlier work, and with a perceptive study of changing social norms – particularly with the question of what makes a gentleman.

Primarily, however, *Persuasion* is a romantic comedy, with a surprisingly mature heroine. "A woman of seven and twenty," says Marianne Dashwood, in *Sense and Sensibility*, "can never hope to feel or inspire affection again." *Persuasion* almost seems written to prove Marianne wrong. Anne Elliot, its heroine, is 27 when the novel opens and is deeply in love – hopelessly, she believes. Eight years before the story opens, Anne had become engaged to Frederick Wentworth, a brilliant young naval officer, ambitious and self-confident, but "with nothing but himself to recommend him."[1] He had no fortune of his own, no influential "connexions" to advance his career – he is unique among Austen's heroes in being essentially a self-made man. Knowing that she could expect nothing from her father, who disapproved of such a marriage, and having no money of her own, Anne had yielded to the persuasion of her intimate friend, Lady Russell, and broken the engagement – not out of concern for herself, but because she feared that such an imprudent marriage could only bring unhappiness to her lover. She loves Wentworth still, but he has never forgiven her for that betrayal, as he sees it, and for the weakness of character that she showed in yielding to persuasion.

With this premise, Austen writes the most romantic of her novels, ending – inevitably – in the reunion of the lovers. "Autumnal" is an adjective that inevitably comes to mind in thinking of *Persuasion*. Imagery of autumn, "that season of peculiar and inexhaustible influence on the mind of taste and tenderness," abounds. That phrase alone, "a mind of taste and tenderness," would establish the uniqueness of this novel. None of Austen's other heroines could be so described. Anne's state of mind on leaving Kellynch, her "desolate tranquillity," is equally suggestive. Yet "autumnal" would be a misleading term to apply to this novel as a whole. In the world of experience, autumn is followed by winter, the season of cold and of death. In *Persuasion* there is no winter, and the novel closes with a renewal of life and energy.

It is tempting to attribute the unique emotional quality of *Persuasion* to Austen's intimations of her own mortality (her health had apparently begun to fail in the spring of 1816). Tempting, but unprovable and unnecessary – if *Persuasion* is entirely different in feeling from *Emma*, so was *Emma* from *Mansfield Park*, *Mansfield Park* from *Pride and Prejudice*, and *Pride and Prejudice* from *Sense and Sensibility*. Austen does not repeat herself – *Persuasion*, the most subjective, the most deeply felt of her works, follows *Emma*, the most comic.

Compared with its predecessors, the development of *Persuasion* is surprisingly slow. It is not until the fourth chapter that readers learn the history of Anne's unhappy love for Wentworth, or even that it has occurred. Emma Woodhouse had already chosen Harriet Smith as her protegé and knows of her interest in Robert Martin by chapter 4 of *Emma*, and Mr. Woodhouse, Mr. and Mrs. Weston, and Knightley have been introduced. In chapter three of *Pride and Prejudice* Elizabeth Bennet overhears Darcy's contemptuous reference to herself – "she is not handsome enough to tempt *me*" – and forms her prejudice against him.

The first three chapters of *Persuasion* present the Elliot family – Sir Walter, the father, and his three daughters. As in *Emma*, the mother died when her daughters were young. Again, as in *Emma*, the father is thoroughly incompetent, though for quite different reasons. His character is created in a single sentence: "Vanity was the beginning and the end of Sir Walter Elliot's character; vanity of person and of situation."

Persuasion is not only the most "romantic" (that is, the most deeply emotional) of Austen's novels, but also the most harshly critical. The life of ceremony and social form, totally without emotional content, is mercilessly satirized in the character of Sir Walter. He seems almost a figure from a morality play – Pride, or Vanity, embodied – pride in his personal appearance (his estate, Kellynch, is filled with mirrors) and pride in his rank (he is a baronet, the lowest level of the aristocracy). Elizabeth, his oldest daughter, is as handsome and as vain as himself. Mary, the second daughter, has a smaller share of the "Elliot pride," just enough to make her "tiresome and helpless." Anne has none at all.

A different sort of pride – in his own ability and accomplishments – is represented by Captain Wentworth. It is not that Austen has become a social leveler but that this novel, more than any of the others, demands that from those to whom much is given, like Sir Walter, much is required. "You misled me by the term *gentleman*," remarks Sir Walter, speaking of Wentworth's brother, a curate. "I thought you were speaking of some man of property" – meaning by "property," an inherited estate. But that simple definition was no longer acceptable, as the context indicates and as Austen clearly expects her readers to agree. "What makes a gentleman?" would become a constantly recurring question throughout the nineteenth century, both in literature and in society. In the world of *Persuasion*, and increasingly in Austen's England, a man could be a gentleman without owning property – that is, land. Wentworth has no estate (although he will no doubt acquire one with his £25,000 of prize money), but his ability and accomplishment, his character and manners make him a gentleman already.

Birth and fortune together (with "fortune" meaning the ownership of land) automatically conferred that privileged status of "gentleman," but where those claims were weak, individual achievement might strongly supplement them. The three admirable male characters of *Persuasion* – Admiral Croft, Captain Harville, and Captain Wentworth – are all naval officers who have distinguished themselves, and all three are clearly gentlemen, equal to any society. The hereditary gentlemen of the novel make a poor showing in comparison – Sir Walter himself, Charles Musgrove, a decent enough fellow who idles his time away in sport while waiting to inherit the family estate, and Mr. William Walter Elliot, the heir to Kellynch, who has grown rich by marrying a rich woman. Not one of them has done anything to justify his position.

As a landowner, Sir Walter Elliot has totally failed in his responsibility. To pay his debts, he is forced to rent Kellynch and go off to Bath – thus abdicating his position, in effect – where he can live a life of pure ceremony, apparently made up of holding and attending receptions and of politely greeting acquaintances of equal rank as he walks the streets. But the effect of his irresponsibility is not limited to his family or his tenants. In mismanaging and abandoning his estate, he has not only disgraced himself but has discredited his class – an idea that never occurs to him. He is the ultimate snob – concerned only with titles, rank, and pedigree, never with the social role that his position should impose on him. He feels no responsibility for the welfare of his tenants and has no concern for passing Kellynch on to his successor in at least as good condition as he had found it when it came to him.

Yet while Sir Walter is an important character, he affects the plot only by renting Kellynch and by moving to Bath and eventually bringing Anne there. He cannot function as a blocking agent – he is too self-concerned to do that. While he had disapproved of Anne's engagement, his opposition had nothing to do with her breaking it, and he makes no attempt to prevent her eventual union with Wentworth. He forms, instead, one half of a dichotomy – embodying the life of Ceremony as opposed to the life of Feeling, in Anne. ("The sameness and the elegance, the prosperity and the nothingness of her scene of life" – those terms describe Elizabeth Elliot's existence, but they apply equally to Sir Walter.) He also, quite unknowingly, launches the action of the novel, bringing Wentworth and Anne together for the first time since their separation, when he leases his estate to the Crofts.

Only in *Persuasion*, among all of Austen's novels, can the period of the action be dated quite precisely. The tenant of Kellynch hall is Admiral Croft, retired from the navy not because of age but because of peace. The long wars with France had just ended, warships were being laid up, and officers and crews put on shore. (In the final lines of the novel, Wentworth says, "Like other great men under reverses . . . I must endeavour to subdue my mind to my fortune. I must learn to brook being happier than I deserve"; contemporary readers would surely have caught the joking reference to Napoleon in exile.)

The Crofts become interesting and entertaining characters in their own right – particularly the dauntless Mrs. Croft, able to manage a carriage or an estate – but their role in the plot is simply to unite Wentworth and Anne again, since he is Mrs. Croft's brother, and he naturally visits her at Kellynch. He, too, is on shore, now wealthy from captures of French ships, but still unmarried and unsettled.

Sir Walter's dislike for the navy might be expected – he is a fool – but one of his reasons is a fine comic surprise, yet entirely consistent with his character: naval service "cuts up a man's youth and vigour most horribly; a sailor grows old sooner than any other man." The other is more predictable – that the navy is "a means of bringing persons of obscure birth into undue distinction" (a phrase that could apply to Wentworth). This again brings up the question, "What, or who, is a gentleman?"

With the renting of Kellynch, the sequence of events begins by which Anne Elliot can be released from the physical and emotional stasis in which she has been held for eight years. Since the reunion of Wentworth and Anne is predictable almost from the outset, the author's problem is to find plausible means of delaying it and keeping the heroine in uncertainty until the final moment. Since heroine and hero are mature adults, since Anne feels no need for her father's approval and Wentworth has gained a comfortable fortune, the barrier between them is entirely psychological – his bitter resentment toward Anne for what he considers to be the weakness of her character or her love in yielding to outside influence ("persuasion") and breaking their engagement instead of boldly risking everything on the future, as he was prepared to do.

"When any two young people take it into their heads to marry," the narrator observes in the final chapter, "they are pretty sure to carry their point," and if so, "how should a Captain Wentworth and an Anne Eliot, with the advantage of maturity of mind and one independent fortune between them fail of bearing down every opposition?" (In fact, Sir Walter finds his new son-in-law acceptable, but his approval is not required.) Since Anne never doubts her unflagging love for Wentworth, the action of *Persuasion* must cause him to recognize his continuing love for Anne, partly through seeing her superiority to the other women he meets, and then to realize that she still loves him. He must, of course, be given cause to doubt her continuing love.

How, then, is the novel to be filled and interest maintained until the final understanding is reached, when the outcome is so easily predictable? By the reader's immersion in the sufferings, the anxieties, the fears, and finally the hopes of Anne Elliot. So Wentworth is attracted (almost forces himself to be attracted) by Louisa Musgrove, while Anne must watch and suffer. A certain poetic justice is inflicted – when he at last acknowledges his love for her, he must fear that it's too late, that she will marry her cousin, William Walter Elliot.

In this "novel of little dialogue," as one Marilyn Butler calls *Persuasion* (Butler, 283), the heroine's point of view must be observed almost as consistently as in *Emma*, although for quite different reasons and with an entirely different effect. Anne Elliot is nearly always right in her judgments and in her actions, while Emma is nearly always wrong. It is this consistency in point of view, this awareness by the reader of the depth of the heroine's feeling, much more than the imagery of fall during the scenes at Lyme, which produces the often-noted "autumnal" tone of *Persuasion* and makes it the most romantic of Austen's novels. Not only Anne's happiness but her beauty seems to have vanished in this premature autumn of her life. "A few years before Anne Elliot had been a very pretty girl," the narrator observes, "but her bloom had vanished early." Yet that "bloom" will return.

One might say that there are three worlds, or three levels of existence, in this novel. The first and lowest is the world of Sir Walter and his eldest daughter – a world of pure ceremony, of form without content. At the opposite extreme is the world of true and deep feeling, the world of Anne and finally of Wentworth. *Persuasion's* endorsement of Anne – her behavior, her feelings, her judgment – seems unequivocal. Between these extremes falls the everyday world of the Musgroves – a comfortable, common-sensible world, not overly sensitive or refined. Their good-hearted mediocrity is surely preferable to the sterile politeness of Kellynch, as Anne recognizes, but its limitations are never ignored. The younger Musgroves often appear like large and unruly children in comparison with Anne.

Much of the action of *Persuasion* necessarily takes place on this midlevel of existence – the Musgrove level, it might be called. It is at Uppercross, the Musgrove estate, that Anne and Wentworth meet for the first time in eight years, and that Wentworth allows himself to become entangled with Louisa Musgrove, and it's on an excursion to Lyme with the Musgroves that Anne is briefly attracted to Captain Benwick. More important, Wentworth is gradually compelled to admit the superiority of Anne Elliot over the Musgrove daughters – both of whom are young and marriageable, and are attracted to him.

Although the terms *sense* and *sensibility* are not used in *Persuasion*, it is clear that Anne possesses both to a high degree, as does Wentworth (although in his relationship to Anne he has allowed resentment to overcome his sense). There is a contrast in *Persuasion* not only between feeling and the entire absence of feeling, exemplified by the difference between Anne and her father and oldest sister, but also between true and false or exaggerated feeling. That quality is displayed by Louisa, but still more by Captain Benwick, as he demonstrates to Anne "his familiarity with all the tenderest songs" of Scott and "all the impassioned descriptions of hopeless agony" of Byron. But as he recites "with tremulous feeling" lines describing "a broken heart, or a mind destroyed by wretchedness," all the while looking "so entirely as if he meant to be understood," readers must suspect, even before his engagement to Louisa, that this appearance of inconsolable grief is merely a pose.

Benwick is obviously a pretender to sensibility, advertising both his devotion to the poetry of Scott and Byron and his supposedly inconsolable grief at the loss of his fiancée, Fanny Harville. This showy grief, which does not prevent him from soon becoming engaged to Louisa, and his ready display of his suffering to an entire stranger like Anne, contrasts sharply with Anne's stoical resignation to her own loss of happiness. He and Louisa are well matched – they are not conscious hypocrites like Mr. Elliot, but are nevertheless playing a role. True feeling, in this novel, makes no outward show. Louisa, in comparison with Anne, seems hardly more than an eager child ("eager" is a word often used to describe her), who insists on having her way at all costs. But for Wentworth, still bitter at Anne's "betrayal" of him, Louisa's is "the character of deci-sion and firmness" – just the qualities that he believes Anne had failed to display at the decisive moment.

In *Persuasion* it is the hero, not the heroine, who must be edu-cated. At Lyme, Wentworth comes to understand that what he had taken for strength in Louisa is actually childish willfulness. As the whole party prepares to come down a steep flight of stone steps, Louisa insists on jumping from step to step with Wentworth catching her as she lands. When she takes her second leap, ignoring his objec-tion (saying, "I am determined I will") and jumping before he is ready, she severely injures herself. Wentworth is overcome by the sense of his own guilt in encouraging her at first, while Charles is helpless, and Henrietta faints – only Anne, whom Wentworth had considered so weak, can advise and act. "No one so proper, so ca-pable as Anne!" he cries. Anne, in fact, occasionally comes danger-ously near perfection. But she is humanized here, by a moment of re-flection in which she wonders whether Wentworth still believes in "the universal felicity and advantage of firmness of character" and whether he might not feel that persuadability could sometimes be a desirable quality.

Louisa's accident at Lyme constitutes the turning point of the novel. As Anne takes charge, her return to active life commences. But even before the accident, her beauty and her power of attraction appear to have returned, together with, and clearly resulting from, the re-turn of her full, long-suppressed passion for Wentworth. For seven years Anne's energy has been devoted to repressing her deepest emotion – now that energy is freed. *Persuasion* presents the rejuve-nation of Anne Elliot. The narrator states directly that Anne's "bloom had faded," and Wentworth, on first seeing her after their eight-year separation, had thought her "wretchedly altered." But Benwick is at-tracted by her at first sight, and so also is the passing stranger – later revealed to have been Mr. Elliot, her cousin – who looks at her "with a degree of earnest admiration, which she could not be insen-sible of" – and cannot help enjoying. More important, Wentworth observes this stranger's admiration and for the first time takes notice of the change in Anne. "She was looking remarkably well," comments the narrator, her face "having the bloom and freshness of youth restored by the fine wind which had been blowing."

This return of Anne's beauty is clearly to be taken as an objective reality, as established not only by the responses of Benwick and Mr. Elliot but by Sir Walter's compliments when they meet in Bath – "less thin in her person, in her cheeks; her skin, her complexion greatly improved – clearer, fresher," with his inquiry as to what lotion she has been using, and by the anonymous lady who remarks, "She is pretty, I think, Anne Elliot; she is very pretty," and who thinks her more attractive than her sister Elizabeth, a recognized beauty. Anne's hope, "that she was to be blessed with a second spring of youth and beauty," is in fact fulfilled.

Anne must still suffer, even after Louisa's accident, but her trials will be of a different sort. The second volume of *Persuasion*, after its two opening chapters, is set primarily in Bath, which as experienced by Anne consists of blank streets and squares and crowded interiors – a world of polite, meaningless conversation, of empty social forms. Bath, much more than Kellynch, is the perfect setting for Sir Walter. It is a world of form without content, of pure externality, of barren, meaningless social rituals – receptions, calls, the leaving and collecting of cards – in total contrast to the rich inner life of the heroine, confident after her first meeting with Wentworth there that "he must love her" still. (In striking contrast to the presentation of Emma Woodhouse, in *Persuasion* Austen's endorsement of her heroine seems unqualified.)

Anne must still suffer, of course. Time after time there will be moments when a complete understanding with Wentworth seems imminent, only to be postponed by some interruption from the external world. Privacy, between unmarried men and women, seems extraordinarily limited in this society. There is difficulty as well in the powerful conventions that prohibited a woman even to hint at her love for a man before she was assured of his – conventions Anne Elliot is too modest to defy.

Austen's first problem, after the scene shifts to Bath, is not to create suspense – an impossibility, when everything indicates a rapidly approaching reconciliation – but to credibly delay that outcome, as at the concert where only Mr. Elliot's interruptions prevent a mutual understanding and reconciliation between the two lovers. The second, and probably more difficult question is how to bring about that reconciliation, when Anne's "delicacy" (meaning, in this context, her feminine modesty) prevents her from volunteering the information that Wentworth is too proud to ask for – that she has no intention of marrying Mr. Elliot.

By a rare stroke of luck, the first version of the reconciliation scene was preserved and can be compared with Austen's final version.[2] According to the author's original intention, while Anne is walking down the street after learning from Mrs. Smith the truth about Mr. Elliot's dissolute life as a young man and the hardness of heart he displayed toward his closest friend, she encounters Admiral Croft, who promptly invites her into his lodgings to meet his wife. She finds Wentworth inside, and the Admiral immediately takes him into an adjoining room for a private conversation, which Anne partly overhears.

The Admiral goes out, Wentworth reenters, and for the first time in the novel, he and Anne are alone together. Wentworth speaks, to communicate the Admiral's message – that in view of her impending marriage to Mr. Elliot, he will surrender Kellynch to them, if that is her wish. Anne's denial is immediate, and so is the reconciliation of the lovers. Wentworth sits beside her, moves closer, and "her countenance did not discourage. It was a silent but a very powerful dialogue; on his side supplication, on hers acceptance. Still a little nearer, and a hand taken and pressed and 'Anne, my own dear Anne!' bursting forth in the fulness of exquisite feeling, – and all suspense and indecision were over." The Admiral reappears with Mrs. Croft, and Anne remains for dinner and for the evening, with the Crofts frequently managing to be absent, allowing Wentworth to explain his doubts and fears when he considers "all the horrible eligibilities and proprieties of such a match" as her marriage to Mr. Elliot. The present concluding chapter follows.

Such a reconciliation scene, if it had been published, would no doubt have seemed adequate, although it gives Anne little more to do than to deny a rumor and then silently accept Wentworth's proposal. The final version is a great deal more than adequate – it is brilliant and unexpected, surely one of the most moving love scenes not only in Austen's novels but in the whole range of English fiction, even though the lovers never speak to each other.

Anne's debate with Captain Harville on the relative constancy in love of men and women – a variation on a traditional theme – allows her to state her deepest beliefs, the values by which she lives, and so in effect to declare her continuing love for Wentworth without violating the convention of feminine modesty. The tension of the scene is heightened by contrasts – between the setting, a crowded reception room, and this deeply personal dialogue, and still more by the contrast between the formality of the language and the strength of feeling implied, as well as by the reader's sense of the unnoticed listener, Wentworth, and the occasional reminders of his awareness, such as the sound of his pen dropping. Wentworth has already reassured Anne of his continuing love with similar indirectness, in expressing his surprise at learning of Benwick's engagement to Louisa, after so quickly forgetting Fanny Harville: "A man does not recover from such a devotion of the heart to such a woman! – He ought not – he does not." Wentworth is the most passionate of Austen's heroes, and next to Knightley the most fully characterized. Necessarily – it would not be easy to imagine an Anne Elliot waiting eight years for an Edward Ferrars or even an Edmund Bertram.

Language becomes more concrete and more colloquial as emotion rises, and Harville offers evidence of books, songs, proverbs in proof of men's superior constancy, then concludes:

> "But perhaps you will say, these were all written by men."
> "Perhaps I shall. Yes, yes, if you please, no reference to examples in books." There follows, surprising yet perfectly appropriate in this context, the most direct statement of sexual discrimination in Austen's work – not as a grievance, but simply as undeniable fact: "Men have had every advantage of us in telling their own story. Education has been theirs in so much higher a degree; the pen has been in their hands."
> "But how shall we ever prove anything?"
> "We never shall."

And so, with Wentworth's letter to Anne, written while she and Harville are speaking, the story moves quickly to its conclusion. But the conclusion of *Persuasion* is significantly different from the conclusions of Austen's other novels. This hero has no home to bring his bride to, apparently no family to introduce her to, unless it is the "family" of his navy friends. He seems a strikingly *modern* man – self-made, without "connections," relying on his own ability for success. Anne, correspondingly, is an independent woman who can accept her lover without any concern for parental approval. That approval is in fact forthcoming, but it is irrelevant. And the sense of security and permanence that a Donwell Abbey or a Pemberley (or even a rectory) might provide, is entirely lacking. Instead, Anne "must pay the tax of quick alarm" for her husband's profession. It is this final uncertainty, perhaps, combined with its intense subjectivity, that makes *Persuasion* seem not only the most romantic but also the most modern of Austen's novels.

Chapter Eight

Fragments

"The Watsons," composed in 1804, and "Sanditon," written in 1817, have a quality in common that is more important than simply being unfinished. Both seem more concerned with wider social realities or social developments than Austen's completed novels – in the case of "The Watsons," with the desperate situation of the poor, unmarried woman in the society of early nineteenth-century England, in "Sanditon," with a loss of social order and stability, as represented by Mr. Parker's efforts to enrich himself by turning an ancient fishing town into a fashionable resort for vacationers and health seekers. But Austen abandoned "The Watsons," presumably because she found the subject uncongenial, and she put aside "Sanditon" because of an incapacitating illness that resulted in her death in July 1817.

"The Watsons"

Emma Watson, a beautiful and intelligent woman of 19, has been raised in luxury in the home of her wealthy, childless aunt. But after her husband's death, the aunt marries a fortune hunter and Emma must return to her father's home. He is an invalid, a clergyman with a small income, who must support four unmarried daughters. There are also two sons, one a prospering lawyer, the other a struggling surgeon. Soon after her arrival, Emma attends a ball in the neighboring town and by a simple act of kindness attracts the attention of the local "Great People" – Lord Osborne and his mother and sister, of Osborne Castle. Accompanying them is Mr. Howard, an unmarried clergyman and Lord Osborne's former tutor, who seems destined to be the hero of the novel. Lord Osborne is described as "a very fine young man," but with "an air of Coldness, of Carelessness, even of

Awkwardness."[1] There is a clear resemblance to Darcy, although his apparent pride appears to be simply the effect of shyness, which disables him in company. It seems likely that Emma was intended to educate him and improve his manners, although not to marry him.

Mrs. Blake, the widowed sister of Mr. Howard, accompanies her brother, together with her 10-year-old son. Miss Osborne has promised to be the boy's partner in the first dance, which he is delightedly anticipating, but she breaks her promise when a smart young colonel offers himself as a partner. Standing by and seeing the boy's bitter disappointment, Emma kindly takes Miss Osborne's place – in an act quite similar to Knightley's rescue of Harriet Smith in *Emma*, when Mr. Elton publicly snubs her at the ball at the Crown inn. Young Charles is delighted, and before the evening is over friendship is established between Emma and Mrs. Blake and her brother, an attractive, single man in his early 30s. Even Lord Osborne condescends to notice her.

Austen revealed her plan for completing the work to her sister, Casssandra: "Mr. Watson was soon to die; and Emma to become dependent for a home on her narrow-minded sister-in-law and brother."[2] She would nevertheless decline an offer of marriage from Lord Osborne, and would eventually marry Mr. Howard. Lord Osborne's sister would also be in love with Howard, adding complications. Osborne is to be rejected, then, but also to be educated by Emma, rather as Darcy is educated by Elizabeth. Before the fragment breaks off, Emma has already begun to teach him how to address a lady – "with a degree of considerate propriety" instead of the "half-awkward, half-fearless" style with which he had opened their conversation.

Although "The Watsons" continues for another 10,000 words or so after the ball scene, the plot hardly begins to develop beyond an unexpected visit by Lord Osborne and his subservient friend, Tom Musgrave, to the Watsons. Rather than moving the action forward, Austen seems to be dramatizing the condition of single women in her society – particularly the terrible pressure to marry and the consequences for a woman of failing to find a husband. It's a subject that she would return to in her novels – in Charlotte Lucas's acceptance of Mr. Collins (a sensible woman deliberately marrying a fool in order to gain a home of her own), and contrastingly in Jane Fairfax's honorable readiness to break her engagement to Frank Churchill when his behavior outrages her, even though marriage to him seems her only alternative to a lifetime of drudgery as a governess.

Margaret and Penelope, two of Emma's sisters, are shameless husband hunters. "There is nothing she [Penelope] would not do to get married," remarks Emma's remaining sister, Elizabeth. Penelope, who "thinks everything fair for a Husband," had turned Elizabeth's lover against her, hoping to steal him for herself. She also has designs on "rich old Dr. Harding" and has "taken a vast deal of trouble about him & given up a great deal of time to no purpose." Margaret, in contrast, relies primarily on an affectation of gentleness to attract men: "continual smiles & a very slow articulation being her constant resource when determined on pleasing."

Even to Elizabeth, who will not openly pursue a man, a proper feminine delicacy is a luxury she cannot afford: "I do not think there *are* many very disagreeable Men; – I think I could like any good humoured Man with a comfortable Income." No Austen heroine ever makes such a remark. Yet Elizabeth, although lacking in "delicacy," is generous: "You are very pretty," she tells her sister Emma, "and it would be very hard that you should not have as fair a chance as we have all had, to make your fortune." Beauty is a poor and single woman's most valuable asset, but a rapidly depreciating one.

The miniature debate between Emma and Elizabeth Watson that follows poses the issue – should a woman marry a man she cannot love to gain a home – and reveals more fully and directly than any passage in Austen's completed novels the intensity of the pressure on women to marry and the miserable consequences of failure. When the naive Emma expresses shock at the thought of pursuing a man simply for the sake of marriage – "Poverty is a great Evil, but to a woman of Education & feeling it ought not, it cannot be the greatest" – and concludes that "I would rather be Teacher at a school (and I can think of nothing worse) than marry a Man I did not like." Her sister's reply is simple: "*I* have been at school, Emma, & know what a life they lead; *you* never have." None of Austen's primary heroines is ever faced with such a choice, although Charlotte Lucas, a secondary character in *Pride and Prejudice*, is confronted with it. While Elizabeth, her best friend, unequivocally condemns Charlotte's decision, the final verdict is ambiguous.

If "The Watsons" had been continued, Austen would probably have proved the strength of her heroine's principles by requiring her to refuse Lord Osborne's proposal before being certain of Mr. Howard. Clearly, in "The Watsons" as in all her novels, the odds are on the side of the men. They make the offers, with women having only the right of refusal. If men do not inherit estates, there are professions in which they can make their way, as do Edmund Bertram, John Knightley, and Frederick Wentworth; and in any case, they do not need to marry. A man has his business, his profession, or his estate, and if he remains a bachelor, he is no object for pity or ridicule. So Tom Musgrave can afford to play the flirt – he has nothing to lose by doing so – but a woman who is taken in by him endangers her chance of finding a husband and a home.

For Emma, a young woman who had been "the Life & Spirit of a House, where all had been comfort & Elegance," who had felt assured of a comfortable home during her aunt's life and on her death of coming into a substantial income, the move back to her father's home provides what must be the severest shock undergone by any Austen heroine. Only in her father's chamber, a sickroom, can Emma be safe from "the dreadful mortifications of unequal Society, & family Discord – from the immediate endurance of Hard-hearted prosperity, low-minded Conceit, & wrong-headed folly."

Telling details would surely have been added in revision – description made wittier and more precise, speech further individualized. But even as it stands, the ballroom scene is effective. Tom Musgrave – a snob and in his own way a rake, although, as with Henry Crawford, emotional rather than physical seduction appears to be his goal – is amusing, and seems a promising antihero. And there are brief descriptions that momentarily resurrect that life of nearly 200 years ago – two women in an open carriage, splashing along a muddy lane on their way to a ball in a neighboring town; details of housekeeping as Elizabeth complains about the "great wash"; the whist club in town where husbands escape from their families for three nights a week. But for modern readers the primary interest of "The Watsons" is likely to be found in its almost grimly realistic documentation of the inequalities of the marriage market and the consequences for women of failure in it. It seems a path clearly incompatible with comedy, which may well account for Austen's abandonment of it.

"Sanditon"

"Sanditon" is one of the most tantalizing fragments in English literature, seeming to promise a radically new departure in Austen's work. In its setting (a fishing village in the process of being transformed into a seaside resort), in its characters (a visionary real estate developer, a family of hypochondriacs, a would-be seducer and his chosen victim, and a coolly objective heroine who observes everything with detached amusement,) and in its apparent theme (a satirical contrast between the solidity of an older England and the insubstantial novelty of a new, as exemplified in the development and promotion of Sanditon), it differs strikingly from any of Austen's completed novels. It foreshadows a major topic of the nineteenth-century English novel – the speculative mania and its consequences, harshly satirized in such works as Dickens's *Our Mutual Friend* (1865) and Trollope's *The Way We Live Now* (1875).

Like "The Watsons," "Sanditon" appears to have a direct social concern, and like *Persuasion*, it recognizes social change. Class distinctions were certainly not disappearing in Austen's England, and the ownership of land still carried much, if not all, of its traditional authority and prestige and would continue to do so throughout the nineteenth century. But a middle class of professional and businessmen was steadily growing in number, wealth, and influence, its members imitating the manners and lifestyle of the gentry as far as they could afford to. Such men and their families, escaping from the city to find health and recreation by the sea, are expected by Mr. Parker to make the builders and tradesmen and lodging-house keepers of Sanditon prosper, while he, as a landowner in the area, grows rich from his rents.

Mr. Parker is the principal developer of Sanditon, attempting to turn a quiet fishing village into a fashionable seaside resort, with emphasis on the miraculous health-giving qualities of sea air and sea bathing. Although one of the gentry himself, a member of a long-established family, he seems a strikingly modern figure, living in a world of publicity and promotion rather than of physical realities. While considering himself a practical man, he is in fact a visionary. Sanditon for him, the narrator tells us, was "his Mine, his Lottery, his Speculation . . . his Occupation, his Hope, & his Futurity."[3] Mr.

Parker is a quixotic figure, ever transforming reality to suit his vision, although unlike Cervantes's Quixote, his motives are largely selfish. But not wholly so – while the term *progress* never actually appears, he is a devout believer in it, defined as real estate development.

He speaks a language of superlatives, of public relations, of advertising that is entirely new in Austen's work. The village of Sanditon, he exclaims, is "the favourite spot of all that are to be found along the coast of Sussex; – the most favoured by Nature, & promising to be the most chosen by Man." He can believe clear contradictions. The sea air and sea bathing, for him, are "healing, softing [*sic*], relaxing – fortifying & bracing – seemingly just as was wanted." His outburst on seeing a pair of blue shoes, the latest fashionable color, in a shop window reveals a comic yet potentially dangerous confusion of values: "Civilization, Civilization indeed! Well, I think I *have* done something in my day." British victories seem to matter to him only as they can be pressed into the service of real estate promotion. The name "Waterloo" (fought barely a year and a half before Austen commenced "Sanditon") is intended for a planned crescent. Mr. Parker believes that "joined to the form of the building" that name "will give us the command of lodgers."

"Sanditon" differs from Austen's other writings not only in theme but in technique. Its opening chapter employs a direct, almost allegorical symbolism: "A Gentleman and a Lady . . . being induced by Business to quit the high road, & attempt a very rough Lane, were overturned in toiling up its long ascent, half rock, half sand." (The business involved is the gentleman's effort to locate a surgeon, whom he believes is living somewhere along this road, and persuade him to move his practice to Sanditon.) The episode itself, the language, the implications, seem clearly allegorical, often reminiscent of John Bunyan's *Pilgrim's Progress*. Certainly in Mr. Parker's rhapsodic description of Sanditon ("Sandy-Town"), Austen might have expected her readers to recall the reference in the New Testament to "the foolish man, which built his house upon the sand" (Matthew 7:26) and to remember its fate: "And the rains descended, and the floods came, and the winds blew and beat upon that house, and it fell, and great was the fall of it."

Significantly, the Parker carriage is overturned on a road bordering the estate of Mr. Heywood (whose name, while realistic, surely carries symbolic weight, with its implications of a way of life rooted in the earth), who is at the moment occupied in overseeing the haymaking. This ancient occupation, one of the bases of life, contrasts sharply with Mr. Parker's futile errand and visionary project. Living in a world of publicity and promotion, he is quickly recognized by the Heywoods as an "imaginist" (a word apparently of Austen's invention) obsessed with the development of Sanditon, blinding himself to reality.

Sanditon appears to be his principal reason for existence, "his Mine, his Lottery, his Speculation . . . his Occupation, his Hope, and his Futurity," yet the entire enterprise appears as misguided as the errand that causes his accident. His enterprise is condemned by his own words – "those good people who are trying to add to the number [of bathing places] are in my opinion excessively absurd, & must soon find themselves the Dupes of their own fallacious Calculations." But the calculations of those rivals can hardly be more absurd than his own, and the collapse of his speculations seems to be assured.

Nothing about Mr. Parker and his plans, or the town itself, suggests security or stability. Sanditon has its beauty, but of a kind that is new to Austen's novels. Here, everything seems light and bright and insubstantial. Instead of a stately home with its grounds and its trees, a Pemberley or a Sotherton, the visitor sees "a miscellaneous foreground of unfinished Buildings, waving Linen, & tops of Houses . . . the Sea, dancing & sparkling in Sunshine & Freshness." The Parkers themselves have abandoned their ancestral home, nestled in a sheltered hollow that protected them from storms, with garden and orchard and trees to shade their house from the sun, for a new house – modishly named "Trafalgar House" – built on a height for the sake of the view and exposed to the full force of every storm. But Mr. Parker argues, with his usual absurdity, that "the Wind, meeting with nothing to oppose or confine it around our House, simply rages & passes on." That contrast between the safety and solidity of the former home and the frightening insubstantiality of the new, exposed to every storm, surely implies a contrast between a traditional, conservative rural England and a new, urban, and recklessly speculative society. The final outcome of "Sanditon" seems at least partly predictable. A collapse of Mr. Parker's speculations seems sure (although probably not to the extent of entirely impoverishing him – he is an amiable, if self-deluded, man). Financial loss might coincide with the destruction of Trafalgar House in a storm, with a chastened Mr. Parker returning to the home of his ancestors.

But to return to the plot as far as Austen developed it, the Parkers, grateful for the hospitality they have received from the Heywoods, take Charlotte, one of the Heywood daughters, with them to pay a visit to Sanditon. After the first two chapters, everything is seen from her point of view. Charlotte seems intended as a heroine, but as far as the fragment continues, she functions purely as an observer – reasonably objective, occasionally satirical, always cool and rational – in contrast to the eccentrics and enthusiasts she encounters. Her impressions appear justified, her judgments carry authority.

Mr. Parker's two hypochondriac sisters are enthusiasts also, as totally absorbed in their own health as their brother is in his plans for Sanditon, shocking the sensible Charlotte with the terrifying remedies they unnecessarily inflict on themselves. Diana Parker, the older sister, seems the most energetic woman in Austen's fiction, although her energy seems entirely misdirected, spent on doctoring herself and her sister, or on managing other people's affairs. Mary Lascelles has consequently called "Sanditon" "a hilarious comedy of invalidism,"[4] but this misplaces the emphasis of the story and overlooks the greater originality of Austen's satire on Mr. Parker and all that he stands for.

The development of "Sanditon" is extraordinarily slow. No completed Austen novel leaves so much uncertainty after 12 chapters. At this point in *Pride and Prejudice*, Jane Bennet has fallen in love with Bingley and Darcy is displaying an interest in Elizabeth, while she (or so she believes) thoroughly dislikes him. After 12 chapters in *Mansfield Park*, the crucial Sotherton episode has already taken place, Henry Crawford is playing his seductive game with Maria Bertram, Edmund has been fascinated by Mary Crawford, and Fanny's love for Edmund has been revealed. But in "Sanditon" readers cannot even be certain that the either hero or heroine has been introduced.

There appears to be a comic antihero in Sir Edward Denham – a novelty in itself – and the mysterious Clara Brereton might have become a secondary heroine. Sir Edward's imagination has been inflamed by too much reading of melodramatic novels (like Mr. Parker, he is an "enthusiast" and an "imaginist"), and he speaks an extraordinary language: "It were Hyper-Criticism, it were Pseudo-philosophy to expect from the soul of high-toned Genius the grovellings of a common mind." Significantly he is a "warm friend" of Mr. Parker's plans for Sanditon. Sir Edward has perversely identified himself with the villains of the novels he reads and is ambitious to become a rake and seducer himself, with Clara as his intended victim. "Sanditon" breaks off with Charlotte's view of him in close conversation with Clara, in a remote corner of Lady Denham's park (Lady Denham is a collaborator of Mr. Parker in the development of Sanditon), where they could reasonably expect to find privacy. Clara has seen through Sir Edward and has no intention of being seduced, the narrator has informed us – why then does she allow herself to be placed in a possibly compromising situation with him? The question remains unanswered.

Unfinished novels by major writers seem to invite completion, and Jane Austen's fragments have not escaped such treatment.[5] Such efforts are bound to fail. An imitator of Jane Austen is unlikely to possess her wit and her powers of invention and characterization, and will find it impossible to imitate her style, which while individual to her is also necessarily the product of a particular time and place.

The difficulties in completing "Sanditon" are even greater than with "The Watsons." When "The Watsons" breaks off, a reader familiar with Austen's work might guess the intended development, even without the summary that has been preserved in family tradition. Emma Watson would suffer, she would undergo further misfortunes, but she would finally marry the man of her choice – probably Mr. Howard, the clergyman, even though Lord Osborne could not be ruled out. But for the heroine to refuse such a brilliant match would establish her disinterestedness. As for Tom Musgrave, the antihero, he is plainly destined to fail ridiculously in everything he attempts.

But we do not have the help of family tradition concerning the intended outcome of "Sanditon." Neither does the title provide help – it was supplied by J. W. Austen-Leigh when he printed selections in the second edition of his *Memoir* in 1871 (where "The Watsons," in its entirety, also first appeared in print). The fragment gives no real clues, as the plot development has hardly begun, except for Charlotte's discovery of a puzzling relationship between Sir Edward and Clara Brereton. Is she hoping to trap him into marriage? That Sidney Parker would have become the antihero is unlikely, but it is

easy to imagine him playing an ambiguous role, in the manner of
Frank Churchill. He is "very good-looking, with a decided air of Ease
& Fashion, and a lively countenance" – words that would exactly fit
Churchill. As for Charlotte, she remains a cool, satirical observer
throughout the fragment. Was "Sanditon" intended as novel without
a heroine? Clara seems to Charlotte to be formed for the role of
heroine – she is poor, beautiful, and mysterious – but if her reputation is to be preserved, that intimate conversation with Sir Edward,
when they believe themselves alone in the park, must be explained.
There is also the question of whether Sir Edward, who is quite foolish, can he be taken seriously enough to play the role of antihero.

The manuscript of "Sanditon" is generally considered to be a
first draft – chapter divisions are indicated, but paragraph divisions
are not, and characters are often referred to by abbreviation (Mr. P.,
Lady D.). There has been revision, but only of detail – words,
phrases, sentences crossed out and overwritten. A written plan for
the entire novel may have existed and been lost, of course, or may
have been so clear in the author's mind that there seemed no need
to write it down. Or, with her steadily failing health, Austen may simply have lacked the energy for the kind of detailed planning that
Emma, for example, must have required. But it seems equally possible that in beginning a novel so different from its predecessors,
Austen was feeling her way, trying to discover where she meant to go
in the process of writing. It is conceivable that "Sanditon" would
have been a radically new sort of novel – a novel without a recognizable heroine or hero. Charlotte Heywood, if not to be matched
with the skeptical Sidney Parker, might simply have returned thank-
fully to the peace and stability of her family's home and traditional
way of life.

But if the plot of "Sanditon" cannot be reconstructed, its theme
appears clear enough. It was to be a satire on "enthusiasm" in general, but particularly as seen in the kind of speculative development
that characterized Sanditon. For Mr. Parker, "It [Sanditon] was his
Mine, his Lottery, his Speculation & his Hobby Horse; his Occupation, his Hope & his Futurity." Advertising, "development," movement for the sake of movement, novelty and change – these are what
Mr. Parker values, they constitute the modernity he worships.

If Austen had given her work a title, it may well have been
"Sanditon" – two of her six novels, *Mansfield Park* and *Northanger*

Abbey, take place names as their titles. But if she had chosen a thematic title instead, as she did in *Sense and Sensibility* and *Persuasion*, then *Speculation*, with its implications of foolhardy risk taking, might have been thoroughly appropriate.

Chapter Nine

Austen and Her Critics

To present-day readers, criticism of Austen in her own period is likely to disappoint in quantity and quality. Novels were likely to be treated condescendingly by educated male critics – poetry was universally regarded as the highest literary form. The novel had been unknown in the ancient world, and the majority of novelists and novel readers were female, and by definition uneducated, since no woman could attend university. If novels were reviewed at all, the work of what was then termed an authoress was almost sure to be taken less seriously than that of an author, and in either case was likely to be praised or condemned according to whether or not the reviewer (always male) found it "improving." Moral vigilance was intensified by 20 years of war that seemed to undermine the traditional certainties of life. Consequently, any literary work that questioned tradition – notably the relationship between the sexes – was sure to be harshly condemned.

Novels were expected to provide both pleasure and moral instruction. Thus a reviewer for the May 1812 *British Critic*, examining *Sense and Sensibility*, condescendingly assures "our female friends" that they "may peruse these volumes with real benefit," finding in them "sober and salutary maxims for the conduct of life, exemplified in a very pleasing and entertaining narrative."[1] Three years later the same journal casually dismissed *Emma* as "amusing, inoffensive and well-principled."[2] The path that female novelists, especially, had to follow was a narrow one. A heroine could be independent, for example, but not dangerously so. A generally admiring reviewer of *Pride and Prejudice* notes Elizabeth's "independence of character," then finds it necessary to assure his readers that it "is kept within the proper line of decorum."[3]

But reviews of contemporary novels were few and generally brief. The only extended public notice of Austen's work during her lifetime was a review of *Emma* in the influential *Quarterly Review*,

published anonymously in 1815 but now known to have been written by Walter Scott. Few novels in Austen's day received such attention. Unlike most reviewers of the time, Scott seems to have been
concerned principally with literary rather than moral values. Taking
the morality of the novels for granted, he gives attention instead to
what seems to him the striking realism of her work, finding that in
contrast to the novelists of the eighteenth century, she is concerned
not only with possibility but with probability. It seemed to him a
realism of the commonplace: her subjects were "not often elegant
and never grand,"[4] her stories were made up of everyday events, and
her characters were equally familiar, drawn principally from "the
middling classes of society" (Scott 1815, 1:64). This fidelity to ordinary life replaces the "wild variety of incidents" or exaggerated
"pictures of romantic affection and sensibility" that novels had traditionally provided (Scott 1815, 1:63).

The praise is carefully considered, but Scott's opinion of
Austen's novels improved with rereading. Nearly 10 years later he offered a remarkable tribute, noting that he had "read again, for the
third time at least, Miss Austen's very finely written novel of *Pride
and Prejudice*. That young lady had a talent for describing the in-
volvement and feelings and characters of ordinary life which is to me
the most wonderful I ever met with." He admires above all her
"exquisite touch which renders ordinary commonplace things and
characters interesting from the truth of the description and the sentiment" – a touch that he himself lacked, although "the Big Bow-
wow strain [action, adventure, heroics] I can do myself like any now
going."[5] Readers and critics, however, preferred the "bow-wow
strain" to exquisite realism. For decades Scott was regarded as the
great novelist of the century, and his works enjoyed a mass popularity that Austen's never approached. Masculine heroism, adventure,
great historical events – such subjects were the mark of a major
writer. Lacking them, Austen's novels seemed to some early reviewers to have no story at all.

But if the critical reviews are disappointing, the opinions of
Mansfield Park and *Emma* held by ordinary readers, reported to
Austen by friends and relatives, provide unique evidence of the public response to her work. Then as now, novel readers wanted first of
all to be entertained, and they were as a rule primarily interested in
the qualities that contributed to their amusement – the plot, the

characters, the dialogue. Inevitably, they responded, as readers still do, to fictional characters as if they were real people, and their responses varied widely. In spite of the author's probable intention, there were those who disliked Fanny Price, found Edmund "cold & formal," were "interested by nobody but Mary Crawford" (*Minor Works*, 431). The "pure morality" (*Minor Works*, 433) of *Mansfield Park* is noted and approved, but that certainly is not the prevailing theme.

The two lengthiest comments ignore moral issues and concentrate on the author's unique realism. "Everything is natural, & the situations and incidents are told in a manner which clearly evinces the Writer to *belong* to the Society whose manners she so ably delineates," writes a Mrs. Pole (*Minor Works*, 437), while for Lady Gordon, everything is so "exactly descriptive, so perfectly natural, that every reader can imagine that she herself has known these people, has taken part in these events" (*Minor Works*, 435). (Not that everyone admired realism – "too natural to be interesting" was how one reader dismissed *Emma* [*Minor Works*, 437].) Already the standard of comparison was *Pride and Prejudice*. Each new novel was compared with it, found equal or wanting in this respect or that. ("Not so *brilliant* as P. & P" [*Minor Works*, 438] – a judgment on *Emma* – is typical.)

Austen's novels were published anonymously during her lifetime, and her public image for the half-century following her death was created by Henry Austen's prefatory "Biographical Notice" of his sister. The portrait is normalized, one might say, by Henry's insistence that Austen had excelled in the traditional female accomplishments – drawing, conversation, even music, and that (as readers might have guessed) she "was fond of dancing and had excelled in it."[6] Clearly she was no "bluestocking" – the scornful contemporary term for a female intellectual. Jane Austen was an authoress – that after all was the reason for the notice – but first she was a lady. Her piety – her "ideological correctness," as it might be called today – is emphasized. Not only had she displayed a truly Christian resignation during her final illness, but "On serious subjects . . . her opinions accorded strictly with those of our Established Church" (*Novels*, 8).

Her brother Henry offered no criticism, except the commonplace that "she drew from nature" (*Novels*, 7), but for a century at
least critical attitudes would be influenced by a passage he quoted
from a letter by Austen to a young nephew, describing her own work
as "a little bit of ivory, two inches wide, on which I work with a
brush so fine as to produce little effect after much labour" (*Letters*,
468), in contrast to his "manly, spirited sketches, so full of life and
spirit" (*Letters*, 429). Ignoring the context – a letter of encourage-
ment to a young beginner – this humorous self-deprecation would
often be taken as the author's considered judgment on her own
novels.

Besides Scott's review, the only other significant notice Austen's
work received on its first publication was Richard Whateley's unsigned review of *Northanger Abbey* and *Persuasion* in the *Quarterly
Review*, published after her death – a "review" that is in fact a general essay on her novels. Following Scott, Whateley emphasizes her
unprecedented realism, her avoidance not merely of impossibilities
but of improbabilities. Whateley was a clergyman as well as a critic,
and ideology – which might be roughly defined as the laws, the
rules, the practices, the beliefs that control relationships in a society – is of course not forgotten in his review. Novels are expected to
support the established moral code and religious doctrines, which
for him are inseparable. "Virtue must be represented as producing,
at the long run, happiness; and vice, misery," but through example
rather than by "any direct attempt at moral teaching." The primary
object remains "*to please.*" "Miss Austen has the merit," he continues, "of being evidently a Christian writer," but this is "a merit much
enhanced . . . by her religion not being at all obtrusive." The novelist's task is to combine moral "instruction" with "amusement," without a self-defeating direct effort at the former. Austen's novels meet
this requirement. Moral lessons "are not offensively put forward, but
spring incidentally from the circumstances," and the reader "is left
to collect them . . . for himself."[7]

Whateley's literary analysis goes beyond Scott's in emphasizing
the careful construction of Austen's novels – they have "that com-
pactness of plan and unity of action which is generally produced by
a sacrifice of probability," yet they contain "nothing that is not probable" (Whateley, 1:95). And he makes a surprising comparison – which, however, would often be repeated – observing that

Austen, like Shakespeare, gives "a dramatic air to the narrative, by introducing frequent conversations; which she conducts with a regard to character hardly exceeded even by Shakespeare" (Whateley, 1:98).

With that review, significant criticism comes to an end for nearly 40 years. The novels remained in print – Austen has never been forgotten – but a liking for them was very much a minority taste in comparison to the mass popularity of Scott. (And unlike the novels of Scott, Austen's work has never had any wide circulation or significant influence outside the English-speaking world.) Her work had distinguished admirers, such as Macaulay, Tennyson, Thackeray, George Eliot, and Matthew Arnold, who is said to have read her *Mansfield Park* once a year to improve his own style. But the reading public, as always, preferred new fiction to old, and with the coming of the Victorian age, there was an abundance to choose from. Austen's audience tended to be an intellectual elite – she could almost be called the writer's writer.

Published criticism was resumed in 1859, with George Henry Lewes's "The Novels of Jane Austen," published in *Blackwood's Magazine*. Lewes praises Austen primarily for technique, describing her as "the greatest artist that has ever written, using the term to signify the most perfect mastery over the means to her end."[8] Amplifying on Whateley's comments, he emphasizes Austen's mastery of the "rare and difficult art of *dramatic presentation*" (Lewes, 1:157), a quality that gives her work an unsurpassed sense of reality. But – there is generally a "but" in the nineteenth-century criticism, no matter how admiring – there are "worlds of passionate existence" that found no place in her life or her work. "She risked no failures by attempting to delineate that which she had not seen" (Lewes, 1:159).

Inevitably there were detractors who required profound emotions and high aspirations from literature. To the romantic temperament, Austen's work has often seemed either unintelligible or repulsive. For Charlotte Brontë, *Pride and Prejudice* offered the reader merely "An accurate daguerreotyped portrait of a commonplace face; a carefully fenced, highly cultivated garden, with neat borders and delicate flowers . . . open country, no fresh air . . . I should hardly like to live with her ladies and gentlemen, in their elegant but confined houses."[9] To such readers, Austen's novels seemed totally lacking in "poetry," or imagination, offering only a superficially accurate reproduction of upper-class English life. Elizabeth Barret Browning found Austen's characters to be "wanting souls," adding that while the novels might be "perfect as far as they go . . . they don't go far."[10] And Emerson, reading *Pride and Prejudice* and *Persuasion* in 1861, found them "vulgar in tone, sterile in artistic invention, imprisoned within the wretched conventions of English society . . . Never was life so pinched and narrow. The one problem in the mind of the writer . . . is marriageableness."[11] Mark Twain would later make a similar point in very different language – in trying to read an Austen novel, he "felt like a bartender entering the kingdom of heaven."[12]

The publication in 1870 of J. E. Austen-Leigh's *Memoir* of his aunt's life finally supplied biographical information to supplement Henry Austen's note to *Persuasion* and *Northanger Abbey*, as well as printing for the first time a selection of Austen's letters. The book was so well received that Austen-Leigh immediately prepared a second edition, this time including "The Watsons," selections from "Sanditon," and the cancelled chapter of *Persuasion*. The *Memoir* provides the basis of all later biographies, but it is very much a product of its time, emphasizing Austen's piety and personal virtues rather than her literary abilities (Austen-Leigh was a clergyman).

It is also significant for prompting a review by Richard Simpson, a Shakespearean scholar, which ranks as the most interesting criticism of Austen in the nineteenth century. Simpson's analysis is close to that of Charlotte Brontë, although leading to a radically different evaluation. "The critical faculty was in her [Austen] the ground and support of the artistic faculty," he observes, referring to the early burlesques.[13] Paradoxically, she learned her realism not by direct observation of life but by recognizing and parodying the unreality of the popular fiction of her day. More specifically, Simpson points out that love can be educational in Austen's novels: Austen "seems to be saturated with the Platonic idea that the giving and receiving of knowledge, the active formation of another's character . . . is the truest and strongest foundation of love" (Simpson, 1:244), although he appears to see this giving as proceeding largely from the man to the woman.

He makes a convincing comparison to Shakespeare – "Anne Elliot is Shakespeare's Viola" (Simpson, 1:256), translated into early nineteenth-century England – and he points out the significant parallel between the debate of Captain Harville and Anne concerning the relative constancy in love of men and women with that of the Duke and Viola on the same topic ("There is no woman's sides / Can bide the beating of so strong a passion / As love doth give my heart"). Simpson makes a suggestive division of Austen's novels into two "trilogies" – first *Northanger Abbey, Sense and Sensibility,* and *Pride and Prejudice,* then *Mansfield Park, Emma,* and *Persuasion,* with the second group offering greater emotional depth, variety, and subtlety in characterization, as well as showing increased care in construction. But the author's sex could never be forgotten – after his high and discriminating praise, Simpson concludes by suggesting that Austen's readers should "recognise her officially as 'dear Aunt Jane' "! (Simpson, 1:265).

With Simpson's essay, serious criticism comes to an end for more than a generation, although the popularity of the novels increased – partly as a result of the *Memoir,* which had made Austen's work appear so eminently safe, in what seemed to many readers a time of dangerously sensational fiction. The novels continued to be reprinted – usually in small volumes, often with illustrations emphasizing the quaint manners and costumes of her already distant period, but her audience had changed. The popularity of the novels may have increased, but they were no longer read and admired by writers and intellectuals.

The writer who would seem most likely to have learned from Austen – Henry James, a writer of social comedy himself and a supremely conscious artist as well as a usually perceptive critic – is disappointing when he comments on her work. His remarks seem both patronizing and obtuse, placing her novels in a lesser, female category. Unlike the fiction of male writers, declares James, her work is not the product of conscious art, although it somehow possesses "a narrow unconscious perfection of form."[14] Her reputation has been inflated by the booksellers, as well as by "editors, illustrators, producers of the pleasant twaddle of magazines," who have profited from "their 'dear,' everybody's dear, Jane."[15] With his emphasis on Austen's limitations, James clearly belongs among the detractors. She left "much more untold than told,' even within her limited range – "Why shouldn't it be argued against her," he asks, that "her testimony complacently ends" just where our curiosity intensifies?[16]

The first distinctively modern criticism of Austen, and the first to accept her unequivocally as a major writer, without damaging reservations, is Reginald Farrer's "Jane Austen," published in the *Quarterly Review* in 1917. Farrer's Austen, a satirist and an artist – "the one completely conscious and almost unerring artist" (Farrer, 2:250) in English fiction – differs radically from the model of propriety offered by her nineteenth-century admirers. "Standing aloof from the world, she sees it, on the whole, as silly" (Farrer, 2:255). Farrer's radical reinterpretation of *Mansfield Park* would have been impossible in the Victorian age – that while technically it is one of the most brilliant of her works, it is drastically weakened by "a radical dishonesty" (Farrer, 2:262), a "constant deliberate weighting of the balance" (Farrer, 2:263) against the Crawfords. It is a judgment that every later critic has had to take into account.

Virginia Woolf's commentary on Austen is somewhat disappointing, coming from a major novelist who was also a critic and a feminist. But novelists who criticize their predecessors are likely to find most sympathetic those whose work most resembles their own, and Woolf is no exception. Her attention is given principally to *Persuasion*, the novel she finds most sympathetic – probably because in its emotional quality it most resembles her own. Imagining the six novels that Austen did not live to write, Woolf suggests that she would have perceived "more of the complexity of human nature," and to accommodate her new insight "would have devised a method, clear and composed as ever, but deeper and more suggestive," for conveying "not only what people say, but what they leave unsaid; not only what they are, but what life is."[17] She would, in other words, have become unmistakably a forerunner of Virginia Woolf.

Publication of R. W. Chapman's edition of Austen's novels (five volumes, with scholarly apparatus, from Oxford University Press in 1923, together with his edition of the collected letters in 1932 and a volume of *Minor Works*, containing the juvenilia and the fragments, in 1954) not only conferred classic status on Austen's work but provided the basis for future scholarship and criticism, steadily increasing in quantity. Chapman corrected textual errors that had crept into earlier editions, he restored the original volume divisions (often, though not always, significantly related to the structure of the novels), he printed "Lovers' Vows" with *Mansfield Park* and reprinted the canceled chapter from *Persuasion*, and even provided a glossary of Austen's English. With this edition, the full acceptance of Jane Austen's work into the canon of English literature had finally been achieved. Critics had already ceased referring to her with polite condescension as "Miss Austen," as had been the rule throughout the nineteenth century. After a few decades as "Jane Austen" she would become simply "Austen," as a male writer is "Dickens" or "James."

As early as the 1930s, Austen criticism was becoming specialized, published in academic journals or by academic presses, written by university professors for their colleagues rather than for the general reader. (The disappearance of the "general reader" has been frequently announced, but in fact Austen's novels continue to be read for pleasure by nonspecialists, as the existence of the Jane Austen Society – primarily made up of such readers – demonstrates.) Critical books on Austen began to appear, notably Mary Lascelles' *Jane Austen and Her Art* (1939), an important, highly detailed examination of the writer's techniques, such as the general "low relief" (Lascelles, 95) of her style, which makes the unexpected exception strikingly powerful – such as Miss Bates's "*dreadful* gratitude."

But while the writer presented by Lascelles was far too intelligent and self-conscious to be patronized in Victorian style as "dear Jane," this Austen seems nevertheless essentially at home in her world. A radically different view, which would prove highly influential, was offered in the same year by D. W. Harding in his "Regulated Hatred: An Aspect of the Work of Jane Austen," appearing in the influential critical journal *Scrutiny*.

Harding's Austen is a writer desperately trying to express her own values without alienating herself from her society – to find, in Harding's words, "the means for unobtrusive spiritual survival."[18] Her dilemma, as a writer, is that "of being intensely critical of people [more accurately, "of the sort of people"] to whom she also has strong emotional attachments" (Harding, 173). The "priggishness" of *Mansfield Park*, about which modern attitudes probably differ most sharply from those of Austen's contemporaries, results from "a curiously abortive attempt at humility" (Harding, 175) – the humility of accepting the moral standards of her day, particularly in her handling of the Crawfords and Henry Crawford's elopement with Maria.

Harding acknowledged that his essay, in underlining features of her work that had commonly been ignored, offered "a deliberately lop-sided view" (Harding, 179) with its assumption of a deep division between Austen and her society. But his view has dominated the work of many later critics, notably of Marvin Mudrick in his *Jane Austen: Irony as Defense and Discovery* (1952), probably the most influential critical study of Austen to appear in the twentieth century. Adopting Harding's thesis and applying it to each of Austen's novels, Mudrick assumes that a biting irony is the distinctive quality of her work, and that the novels have integrity only insofar as they maintain this hostile stance toward her society, with its rigid class system, its materialism, and its repressive morality.

But the period from the late 1930s to the 1970s is remembered primarily as the era of "New Criticism" – a criticism primarily concerned (at least in theory) with purely aesthetic values and with detailed analysis of the techniques by which the desired effects were created. An excellent example is Reuben Brower's essay, "Light and Bright and Sparkling: Irony and Fiction in *Pride and Prejudice*" (1951). Brower's purpose, announced at the opening of his essay, is to read the novel "as sheer poetry of wit, as Pope without couplets." Accordingly, he examines the "antitheses," "the play of ambiguities," "the orchestration of tones," the process through which "the ironies of the dialogue function in the curve of the main dramatic sequence"[19] – irony is highly valued by the New Critics.

For Brower, "The triumph of the novel . . . lies in combining such poetry of wit with the dramatic structure of fiction" (Brower, 62). Austen's characters appear essentially timeless in his criticism, their behavior determined by their individual psychology – which in his reading appears to bear some relation to literary convention but to be quite unconditioned by social reality. Such criticism must be (as Brower's is) sensitive to nuance and implication, to the variety of feeling conveyed to readers through the interplay of dramatic dialogue and authorial comment, demonstrating this interplay through careful analysis of selected passages. Brower's Austen is above all a master of her craft, ironic and aloof – except in dealing with Lydia's elopement, when moral outrage becomes too great for irony.

Such criticism would eventually be condemned for deliberately overlooking the realities of class and of power (and in so doing actually collaborating with the existing power structure) in order to concern itself with such topics as irony, style, structure, and literary influences – as though literature existed quite independently of actual social structures and social conditioning. In fact, that condemnation is a considerable oversimplification of a period strongly influenced by Marx and Freud, in which critics often examined both the psychological and social origins and effects of literature.

By the early 1970s, such concerns were beginning to dominate criticism and scholarship, including of course that concerned with Austen's novels. Alistair Duckworth's *The Improvement of the Estate: A Study of Jane Austen's Novels* (1974) placed ideology firmly in the foreground of Austen studies, emphasizing the social and political relevance of her work to her own time. Assuming that *Mansfield Park* is fundamental to Austen's thought, Duckworth takes the "estate" as a symbol of the established order as whole – language, manners, the moral code, the class system – with "improvement" suggesting some change in the relationship of the individual to this heritage. Austen's Toryism is moderate, it does not imply a resistance to change at all costs – rather, while irresponsible action such as Henry Crawford's plans for "improving" Sotherton is to be ridiculed or condemned, authority must regularly be renewed and regenerated, perhaps as Darcy's authority will be regenerated by Elizabeth's energy and wit. But established certainties appear less certain in the later novels. *Persuasion* (with its literal abandonment of the estate) implies a dangerous threat to both moral and social stability.

Marilyn Butler's *Jane Austen and the War of Ideas* (1976) – probably the most influential single work since Mudrick's – concerns itself with "ideology" in a more abstract sense. Basing her conclusions on thorough research into the polemical writings of Austen's day, as well as its fiction, Butler classifies Austen as a moderate "anti-Jacobin" – that is, as a writer whose work essentially upholds the established social order against the subversive ideologies of revolutionary France, and in particular against Mary Wollstonecraft's notorious *Vindication of the Rights of Women* (1792). Readers of Austen's time would not have been surprised by such a discovery – to instruct while giving pleasure was the proper function of novels, just as it was of poems and plays, and vigilant reviewers were prepared to denounce any book that could be read as subverting traditional moral, political, and religious certainties. The ideological critic can appear blind to aesthetic considerations, as in Butler's charge that Austen's novels are seriously incomplete in their presentation of human nature – emphasizing rationality, self-control, and deliberate choice, while disapproving of sensuality and irrationality of any sort. Such a criticism not only oversimplifies the novels – certainly the "irrational" is present throughout Austen's work – but overlooks the fact that Austen is primarily a writer of comedy. Nevertheless, in the light of such scholarship as Butler's, no critic could reasonably claim that Austen's novels exist in some purely "aesthetic" realm, quite apart from the actual world in which they were written.

To Butler and to critics influenced by her work, Austen seemed insufficiently radical in her presentation of relationships between men and women, accepting and therefore tacitly justifying the existing sex roles and the resulting enormous differences in status and power between the sexes. Plainly, she was no Mary Wollstonecraft and her novels constituted no guide to the rights of women, although her heroines do insist on their right to marry only the man that each of them loves. But the matter is not as simple as that. For a woman to become a novelist was a highly significant action in itself, regardless of her own social attitudes and opinions. Publication meant entering the public world, traditionally the sphere of men, and was still considered by conservative males to be an unwomanly act, unsuitable to both female modesty and female abilities. (It also meant earning money rather than inheriting it or receiving it from a husband.) For a woman to publish, for an audience of both sexes, was to claim intellectual equality with men, an equality often denied in Austen's day but taken for granted throughout her novels.

Ideology is inescapable, of course. It is stated or implied in every literary work, and such works cannot be fully understood unless it is taken into account. But while "aesthetic" or "literary" qualities cannot exist in isolation, they nevertheless are real and account for the fact that of the hundreds of novels produced in England during Austen's lifetime, scarcely any besides her own, and perhaps a half-dozen of Scott's, are now likely to be read by anyone except literary scholars. Readers turn to novels not so much to confirm their own beliefs or prejudices as for essentially literary reasons – above all, for the pleasure of entering and experiencing a favorite writer's imagined world.

Since the publication of *Sense and Sensibility* in 1813, Austen's work has always found its audience, and continues to do so – but only in English-speaking countries. During her own lifetime, Great Britain produced two writers, Scott and Byron, whose influence on world literature has been enormous. Austen's, in comparison, seems almost undetectable. Translations of her novels into French appeared during the final years of her life and immediately after her death, but their circulation was apparently minimal. Her work has been continually read and admired in the United States by a select minority, but its effect on American literature has been slight. The fiction of Henry James, given his concern for craftsmanship and the important, often dominating, role played in his fiction by women, might be expected to show her influence, but in fact does not. A heroine like Isabel Archer, in James's *The Portrait of a Lady* – young, energetic, expecting much from the world – might seem to have a good deal in common with Austen's Elizabeth Bennet. But Isabel's enormous ambition – to encounter, to experience, to absorb European manners, history, and culture – and her misguided effort to achieve her goal through marriage to Gilbert Osmond stand in total contrast to the comparatively precise and limited aspirations of Elizabeth, or of any Austen heroine.

Even in English literature, the influence of Austen's work has been slight. It is hardly perceptible in the major novelists, male or female. E. M. Forster admired the social comedy of her novels, and his own work, particularly the early books – *Where Angels Fear to Tread, A Room with a View* – has been compared with hers, but in Forster there is a vagueness quite alien to Austen, a sense of aspirations and of feelings that can never really be stated or satisfied. Perhaps Austen's truest literary descendant – almost the only one – is Barbara Pym. The typical protagonist of a Pym novel might be described as the Austen heroine in an alien world – middle-aged, single, and lonely, usually poor but consciously a "gentle-woman," frequently involving herself in the work of the Church (Anglican), often hoping and always failing to marry. And not only are the Austenian certainties lacking – so is the Austenian wit. Perhaps the wit is impossible without the certainties.

It appears unlikely, then, that Austen's novels will significantly influence future writers except in the most general way – imparting a taste for subtle irony, for example. But it seems very likely that they will continue to be read. Where else can readers find such a witty and spirited heroine as Elizabeth Bennet, such a devastating ironist as Mr. Bennet, such a fool as Mr. Collins – or a more moving love scene than Anne Elliot's indirect declaration of her continuing love for Wentworth, or passion more intense than Marianne's for Willoughby? Or a technical tour de force to surpass *Emma?* And where else a more sober and realistic assessment of human limitations and possibilities than in the narrator's comment, following Emma's acceptance of Knightley's proposal: "Seldom, very seldom, does complete truth belong to any human disclosure; seldom can it happen that something is not a little disguised, or a little mistaken; but where, as in this case, the conduct is mistaken, the feelings are not, it may not be very material."

Chapter Ten

Austen's Comedy

"What is all this about Jane Austen?" a bewildered Joseph Conrad wrote to his friend H. G. Wells in 1913. "What is there *in* her?"[1] Certainly Conrad has not been alone in his puzzlement. A list of Austen's apparent deficiencies can seem crippling. The society her novels present can appear hopelessly narrow and restrictive. It can be argued that her plots are repetitious, that her characterization is superficial, that there is no passion in her work. Her novels, in a sense, are fairy tales – the Cinderella motif is certainly apparent in *Mansfield Park* and *Pride and Prejudice* – set in an ideal rural England that never really existed. Her work is distorted by its conformity to the oppressive social and moral conventions of her time, a conformity that prevents her from working out the logical conclusions of her situations. Instead of working to subvert the harsh and restrictive social, political and religious codes of Austen's day, her novels support it, directly or by implication.

The stories are always told from the point of view of a small and privileged class – the "lower orders," the vast majority of the English people in her day, are hardly seen at all. Even the middle class of professionals, businessmen, and prosperous farmers is largely absent, represented only by the vulgar but kind-hearted Mrs. Jennings in *Sense and Sensibility;* by Mr. Gardiner, Elizabeth Bennet's uncle, who lives in the shadow of his own warehouses; by Robert Martin – Harriet's suitor in *Emma* – who is often referred to but never seen; and by Mr. Shepherd, the sly attorney who is Sir Walter Elliot's man of business in *Persuasion*. Except for John Knightley, a younger son who must earn his living as a lawyer because his older brother inherits Donwell Abbey, Austen's gentlemen appear to have only two acceptable means of employment open to them: the church and the navy.

The subordinate position of women is accepted without protest. The heroine is always a marriageable young woman of the upper

class – a "lady" in the terminology of the day – who must marry because it is the role of women to marry, and this society has no place
for the unmarried woman, although it can easily accommodate a
wealthy widow, a Lady Catherine (*Pride and Prejudice*) or a Lady
Russell (*Persuasion*). Mrs. Smith, in *Persuasion*, is the embodiment
of the unattached, unsupported woman – widowed and sick, without money or family or friends, until Anne Elliot comes to her aid.
(The only fate worse for a woman would be to go on the street, a situation Austen could never have presented, although it is hinted at in
Pride and Prejudice, after Lydia's elopement with Wickham.)

The emotional range of Austen's novels can seem as limited as
their social range. There is, it has often been charged, no strong
feeling, no passion, anywhere in her work. Her craftsmanship may be
exquisite, but the result is trivial, as Austen herself once wryly remarked when describing her typical novel as a miniature, an inscrip-
tion on a two-inch piece of ivory.

For a substantial number of readers, then, the answer to Conrad's question, "What is there in her?" – would be, "Nothing at all."
Or at most, a relaxing escape from the confusion of the modern
world into a simplified and idyllic past. Yet after nearly 200 years
Austen's work continues to be more widely read than that of any of
her contemporaries – read not only by scholars and specialists but
by the intelligent general reader in search of pleasure. It is certainly
true that her novels offer escape, but so does any story, true or
imagined. If it interests us and holds our attention, it necessarily
takes us out of our own world, whatever that may be, into one that
may be more exciting, more amusing, more tragic, or more pathetic,
at any rate more eventful than our own.

To answer Conrad's question, we might begin by constructing what
could be called Austen's own poetics of the novel – although she
would never have used so pretentious a phrase. The materials may
seem scanty, but the "Plan of a Novel, according to hints from various quarters," written by Austen in 1816, can provide a starting
point. The "Plan" burlesques the melodramatic and sentimental
fiction of her day – novels of a kind that some contemporary readers
might have preferred her to write.

The heroine of such fiction must be literally faultless –
"perfectly good, with much tenderness & sentiment, & not the least

Wit" (*Minor Works*, 428). (Wit is a potentially subversive quality, particularly in a woman.) Unlike any Austen heroine, she will be totally submissive to parental authority. When a man tries to propose to her, she will immediately refer him to her father, "exceedingly angry he should not be first applied to" (*Minor Works*, 430). She will possess all of the fashionable female "accomplishments," again unlike Austen heroines, while her father will be "perfect in Character, Temper & Manners" (*Minor Works*, 428) (a satisfactory parent is not to be found in any of Austen's novels). There will be no ambiguous, mixed characters, such as Mary Crawford or Frank Churchill – the wicked will be "completely depraved & infamous" (*Letters*, 429). Kidnappings, escapes, and rescues, moral perfection and villainy, dutiful and universally accomplished heroines – those were the conventions of popular fiction (of the Gothic novel, for example) – conventions Austen chose not to follow.

A different sort of insight is provided by her letters to Anna Austen, a young niece who was writing a novel (apparently never completed) and submitting chapters to her aunt for criticism. Austen demands realism based on experience. Anna is discouraged from sending her characters to Ireland because she knows "nothing of the manners there" (*Letters*, 395). But while presentation of "manners" – speech and behavior – must be accurate, minute descriptions of setting are to be avoided. A writer must not "give too many particulars of right hand & left." "Grouping," as it might be called, is highly important: "you are now collecting your People delightfully . . . 3 or 4 Families in a Country Village is the very thing to work on" (*Letters*, 401). (A close description of *Emma*, her own most recently completed novel.) Clichés, such as having a character plunge into a "vortex of dissipation," must be cut: "I cannot bear the expression; – it is such thorough novel slang – and so old, that I dare say Adam met with it in the first novel he opened" (*Letters*, 404). (Austen's stylistic self-consciousness is shown in her definitive characterization of *Pride and Prejudice*, in a letter to Cassandra shortly after its publication, as "light, and bright, and sparkling" [*Letters*, 299], in consequence of the "playfulness and epigrammatism of the general style" [*Letters*, 300].)

Austen qualified that apparent self-praise by implying that the sparkle was too continuous (few readers would agree), that something heavier, more serious was needed to right the balance. But the stylistic variety of her work is greater than Austen herself acknowledged and than many critics have recognized. Particularly noticeable is the influence of Samuel Johnson on both the prose style and the moral attitudes of the novels. Her description of Wentworth's reversal of attitude toward Anne Elliot and Louisa Musgrove, after the accident at Lyme, provides an unmistakable example: "There, he had learnt to distinguish between the steadiness of principle and the obstinacy of self-will, between the darings of heedlessness and the resolution of a collected mind." Not only is the seriousness, the moral weight, of the passage Johnsonian, but so is the form – in its vocabulary, its balance and parallelism, and its careful discriminations. The moral weight, in fact, depends on just those qualities.

Austen was far from being the "unlearned and uninformed female" (*Letters*, 452) that she called herself with mock modesty in a letter to the Prince Regent's chaplain. In particular, she was well-read in the English novel, not yet 100 years old when she wrote her earliest work and not yet accepted into the higher reaches of "literature." Her spirited defense of the novel and novelists in *Northanger Abbey*, with its claim that "the greatest powers of the mind" can be displayed in novels, is well-known, and the examples that she cites – "Cecilia or Camilla, or Belinda" – are particularly significant as being novels written by women that are primarily concerned with the interests and feelings of women.

It can be argued that not only has Austen – as a female writer – suffered from discrimination but so has the literary mode in which she expressed herself. Comedy has been the victim of prejudice, consistently underrated in contrast to allegedly "higher" forms of literature. ("Aware of her limitations," writes one hostile critic, Austen "confines herself to comedy."[2] Why not say "Aware of her abilities"?) Henri Bergson's observation, in his influential essay "Laughter," that "the comic demands . . . a momentary anesthesia of the heart" and that consequently its appeal "is to the intelligence pure and simple,"[3] is a similar misjudgment. Comedy of course arouses smiles and laughter, as all of Austen's novels do, but feeling is essential as well. A comedy is generally a love story, and while the actions of the lovers may seem absurd, their emotions as a rule will not. The "happy endings" of comedy (including Austen's), which sober critics may condemn as unrealistic, are in fact essential to the form, required by the expectations that it creates.

When one speaks of the comedy of Shaw or Shakespeare or Austen, what comes to mind is not only particular witty lines and amusing situations but something broader – striking individual figures, recurring character types (Austen's antiheroes, for example), characteristic actions and concerns and emotional states. Every writer of comedy creates his or her own comic world, and each of these worlds is unique – though all of them necessarily bear an affinity both to the "real world" of daily experience and to one another. *Northanger Abbey, Emma, Persuasion* – different as these novels seem – are unmistakably products of the same imagination.

The social range of Austen's novels may seem extremely narrow, but in fact this narrowness hardly matters. She does not repeat herself. Every novel has its distinctive tone (compare *Pride and Prejudice* with *Mansfield Park, Persuasion* with *Emma,* or *Emma* with *Pride and Prejudice,* and her characters are never interchangeable from novel to novel. They are not mere types (young lovers, tyrannical fathers, etc.) Every antihero, every fool, is an individual, even every heroine and hero (much rarer in comedy). Darcy would not do as a husband for Emma, or Anne Elliot as a wife for Knightley. *Pride and Prejudice* is not the typical Austen novel – there is no such thing – and Elizabeth has no more claim to be considered the representative Austen heroine than Fanny Price or Anne Elliot.

A village, or a countryside, with usually at least one family whom the heroine can visit – except for the Bath scenes in *Northanger Abbey* and *Persuasion,* this is the representative background of Austen's novels. Into this narrow setting enter one or more outsiders, whose appearance initiates the major action – Willoughby in *Sense and Sensibility,* Darcy and Bingley in *Pride and Prejudice,* the Crawfords in *Mansfield Park,* Frank Churchill in *Emma,* Wentworth (actually making a reappearance) in *Persuasion.* Such characters may function as either hero or antihero, and in either case will seek the hand of the heroine – or of the hero, in the case of Mary Crawford. Frank Churchill only pretends to court Emma, but that pretense arouses Knightley's jealousy and leads him to recognize his own love for her.

The hero must be born and educated as a gentleman, he must have (by the time of marriage) assurance of a sufficient income. Unlike the antiheroes, he must be guided in his conduct by clear moral principles. He must be what he appears to be and must reveal what he is. "Openness" is a major virtue, and cleverness and charm cannot substitute for principle – in fact, masculine charm suggests insincerity. This moral standard allows no compromise – the antiheroes must be rejected, attractive as they may seem. None of them has a clear and firm moral code, none of them appears to have strong, unshakable sense of personal identity. All of them are role players.

Austen clearly believed that the virtues of her heroines and heroes depended on religious faith (they are "Christian morals in a temperate English version," as Graham Hough observes,[4] but while she no doubt assumed such belief in her readers, it is not required as long as the principles themselves, or the consequences of their absence, are convincingly dramatized. Austen is a moralist, but not a punitive one – her comedy as a rule does not suffer from the infliction of a too rigid "poetic justice." Other than being rejected, the only punishment inflicted on the antihero is to go on being himself. At most, in the cases of Willoughby and both Crawfords, he or she may suffer occasionally from a sense of loss.

The country village and the country house offer the most favorable setting for the values of the novels – "principle," "delicacy" (meaning a sensitivity toward and consideration for others – most conspicuous in Knightley), and openness. Such settings create artistic requirements. The number of characters must be limited, and of course the variety of social and human types. Consequently, Austen's characterization is an art of careful discrimination, convincing readers of the reality and importance of often subtle differences. The novels are essentially dramatic. Characterization is achieved and the action advanced primarily through dialogue rather than narration. In comparison with the novels of Samuel Richardson, whom Austen greatly admired, or to those of her Victorian successors, description and analysis are strikingly absent.

The range of speech patterns in Austen's work may seem very limited, especially compared with that of a Dickens or a Joyce, but as Mary Lascelles points out, the "low relief" of Austen's dialogue – its comparative formality and its relatively limited vocabulary – allows individual qualities, such as the directness of Knightley, the vulgarity of Anne Steele, or the pretentiousness of Mrs. Elton, to stand out sharply (Lascelles, 95). Consequently, as Hough notes, the reader "almost unconsciously registers the speech of the characters as natural, affected, pompous or vulgar" (Hough, 224) without any external information whatever as to the actual usage of the time. The standard of proper speech is set within each novel, primarily by the heroines and to a lesser extent the heroes.

As a matter of historical fact, as Hough suggests, the linguistic reality on which Austen bases her dialogue must have been "the middle range of moderately educated speech" – specifically the speech of "the feminine half of the upper bourgeoisie of her time" (Hough, 225). (Only with Anne Steele, in *Sense and Sensibility*, does Austen present a semiliterate character.) Readers of a later time can recognize the intended effects because they will inevitably compare the speech of an Anne Steele or a Mr. Elton or a Miss Bates with "a standard set or implied within the work itself" (Hough, 205). The social attitudes of the novels reflect the attitudes of the same group. (Although Hough adds a significant qualification, that Austen "is far too active a writer to merely 'reflect' anything" (Hough, 225), and still another reservation needs to be made – that it is always tempting to oversimplify the past, to assume that everyone felt and thought in the same way at a particular time.) That moral and social code, as such, no longer holds, but many of its elements seem essential to any society, and as a rule Austen dramatizes the consequences of any breach of the code so effectively that readers can easily accept the implied moral judgment.

Characters are commonly fixed in their location. They cannot avoid one another – Emma *must* go on seeing Mr. Elton after the mutual embarrassment caused by his proposal, Fanny Price cannot escape from Crawford's unwelcome courtship, Anne Elliot, in Bath, cannot avoid her cousin Mr. Elliot. They must interact until the situation has been resolved in some way and the nature of all parties concerned has been fully revealed. (Mobility in fact can give ground for suspicion, as with Henry Crawford; Bingley's status is lower than Darcy's in large part because he has no place of his own.) Confined relationships, together with the effect of the outsider upon them, make up the substance of the novels.

The range of possible actions is equally limited. Men hunt and supervise their estates, women care for children and manage their households, but we do not see these things being done. Personal relationships are the concern of the author, and therefore it is necessary that her characters should belong to a class that enjoys the leisure in which to cultivate those relationships. We see the social occasions, the dinners, the games of cards, the visits, and particularly the balls, so important in Austen's novels (and no doubt in historical reality) as a place for men and women to meet and to fall in love – Catherine and Tilney, Elizabeth and Darcy, Jane and Bingley, all meet at a ball, while Emma and Knightley realize each other's desirability during the ball at the Crown. In the fragmentary "Watsons," too, the heroine draws the attention of the probable hero by an act of kindness she performs at a ball.

Every Austen novel deals with the heroine's finding of a suitable husband, and she follows convention in ending her story with marriage. The fate of the unmarried woman is to be dreaded, as we see from the open desperation of Anne Steele, the hidden anxiety of Elizabeth Elliot, the readiness of an intelligent woman like Charlotte Lucas to prefer even Mr. Collins to spinsterhood. The choice of a husband, then, determines a woman's life, and must be made out of love. For the arranged marriage, Austen expresses biting contempt: "It was a very proper wedding. The bride was elegantly dressed – the two bridesmaids were duly inferior . . . her aunt tried to cry – and the service was impressively read by Dr. Grant." That description alone would guarantee that this marriage, of Rushworth and Maria, will prove disastrous.

To society, marriage appears as primarily a social contract; to the heroines, it is first of all an intimate relationship. Austen's heroines resist all social pressures to marry the wrong man, and overcome all obstacles in the way of marrying the right one. Since the novels are comic, the heroine always prevails – even the timid Fanny successfully resists Henry Crawford's courtship – in defiance of her formidable uncle, Sir Thomas. "Society" is never seen as a monolithic enemy. Lady Catherine may threaten Elizabeth with "the contempt of the world", but Elizabeth knows that Lady Catherine is not the world. Social pressures are real in comedy, but a determined heroine can defeat them.

The novels are concerned with love – the "happy ending" must not seem a mere formula – and feeling can be deep, even though

love scenes may be comparatively few and passion must be con-
trolled by sense. (The object of passion, that is, must deserve such
feeling, as Frederick Wentworth clearly does, in spite of his unjusti-
fied rejection of Anne, and as Willoughby just as clearly does not.)
Comedy, as we have seen, must not be always comic, and Austen
wrote neither farce nor satire, though her comedy contains elements
of both. Surely readers and spectators do care for such figures as
Shakespeare's Viola in *Twelfth Night*, Shaw's Eliza Doolittle in *Pyg-
malion*, or Austen's Emma. There are limits, of course – the
"sentimental comedy" of the eighteenth century is no comedy at
all – but some degree of concern is essential.

Comedy need not, in fact should not, exclude feeling. Certainly
the emotional range of Austen's work has been underestimated.
"Before the house-maids had lit their fire the next day, or the sun
gained any power over a cold, gloomy morning in January, Marianne,
only half dressed, was kneeling against one of the window-seats . . .
and writing as fast as a continual flow of tears would permit her." It
would be absurd to claim that the writer of that passage could not
express deep feeling. And yet readers of *Sense and Sensibility* are often invited to laugh at Marianne. Emma, too, is surely a comic figure,
absurd in her conceit and her mistakes, but there is nothing laughable in her self-recognition – "The blunders, the blindness of her
own head and heart! . . . she was wretched, and should probably
find this day but the beginning of wretchedness." And *Persuasion* is
suffused with emotion. It is precisely Anne Elliot's distinction, her
qualification for the role of heroine, that she is able to feel more
deeply, more lastingly, and more intelligently than any other character in the novel.

Self-analysis – practiced only by the heroines, except in Darcy's
letter to Elizabeth – can be highly important, as in Emma's final
recognition of her own follies, but dialogue is Austen's primary
method of characterization, accounting largely for the "dramatic"
quality so often noticed by the early critics. (The actual proportion of
dialogue to narrative and description is certainly greater in Austen
than in any of her contemporaries.) Individual idiosyncrasies
occur – Anne Steele's bad grammar, Mr. Collins's polysyllabic
vocabulary and cumbrous sentences, Mr. Elton's recurring "Exactly

so," Mrs. Bennet's regular references to her "poor nerves" – but they are never found in the language of the heroine or the hero, which becomes distinctive through the content (Elizabeth Bennet's wit, Knightley's bluntness) rather than the habits of speech.

Vigorous physical action, except in ballroom scenes, is uncommon – so rare in fact that the few examples in Austen's work can easily be listed: Marianne's fall while running downhill and Willoughby's carrying her home afterward, in *Sense and Sensibility*; Elizabeth Bennet's walk across the fields, jumping over puddles and stiles, when Jane is sick at Netherfield; Louisa Musgrove's accident on the steps at Lyme in *Persuasion*. The novels are concerned almost entirely with states of mind and of feeling – for some readers, consequently, there is no "action" at all in them.

Yet analysis of character and feeling is limited almost entirely to the heroines (the single chapter of *Emma* that is narrated from Knightley's point of view is a rare exception). Dialogue is primary in the novels, but Austen has another and highly effective method of characterization, which can advance the action as well. Referred to as "free indirect discourse" or "free indirect style," it provides a highly effective and economical means of presenting the essence of a character's speech (and therefore of his or her personality). It occurs, as defined by Hough, when the actual words of a character are used, "but embedded in the narrative," rather than set off by quotation marks, "and with the grammatical forms assimilated to those of reported speech" (Hough, 225). Such "indirect discourse" can carry all the individuality of full quotation. In the English novel, Austen is a pioneer in its use.

Mr. Elton's proposal to Emma provides an example: as soon as their coach is under way, she finds him "actually making violent love to her: availing himself of the precious opportunity, declaring sentiments which must be already well known, hoping – fearing – ready to die if she refused him; but flattering himself that his ardent attachment and unequalled love and unexampled passion could of having some effect." Those phrases are surely meant to be taken as a selection from Elton's own words, even though they are not enclosed in quotation marks. The technique is economical and forceful – Elton's absurdity is emphasized without risk of its becoming tiresome.

The strawberry picking at Donwell Abbey, again in *Emma*, provides an example of a rather different sort – what might be called collective discourse. "The best fruit in England – every body's favourite – always wholesome. . . every sort good – hautboy infinitely superior – no comparison – the others hardly eatable. . . delicious fruit – only too rich to be eaten much of. . . glaring sun – tired to death," etc. Mrs. Elton dominates (she was "very ready to lead the way"), but there is no need to identify the speakers. If we are meant to assume that it is actually Mrs. Elton who is speaking throughout the passage, then she becomes momentarily representative of the group experience. The technique is comic and again highly economical in its careful selection. It may seem a comic tour de force, existing for its own sake, but it surely creates a powerful impression of the physical reality of the occasion.

The technique is not limited to the comic. As *Emma* nears its end, with its heroine finally realizing her blunders and their possible consequences for her own happiness (including Knightley's possible marriage to Harriet), Austen presents her state of mind through indirect discourse rather than psychological analysis, thus gaining powerful effects of immediacy and authenticity: "She had herself been first with him for many years past. She had not deserved it; she had often been negligent or perverse," etc. But the process of self-discovery is only beginning – Emma concludes that "Could she be secure of that, indeed, of his never marrying at all, she believed she should be perfectly satisfied." And a page further on she sees her whole life as blighted: "All that were good would be withdrawn . . . what would remain of cheerful or of rational society within their reach?. . . How was it to be endured?" Here the technique provides a sense of authenticity that no authorial analysis could equal – essential if Emma's "reformation," or self-recognition, is to seem acceptable.

Heroines, heroes, parents (generally inadequate), antiheroes (and one antiheroine, Mary Crawford), fools, and miscellaneous supporting figures – these are the recurring figures in Austen's novels, although considering the variety of her heroines, it would be more accurate to say that the term *heroine* describes a role rather than a character type. In comparison with the work of such novelists as Fielding or Dickens, it seems a narrow range – a fact that probably accounts for much of the underestimation of Austen's work. But if the types are comparatively few, that hardly matters when almost every character is strongly individual. Consider, for example, the variety among a character type, such as the fools, or an occupational group, Austen's clergymen. But what no doubt seems the greatest novelty in her work to many contemporary readers is that every heroine is distinct and precisely adapted to the novel in which she appears. Heroines in earlier fiction, and in many Victorian novels as well, seem interchangeable. Critics can speak of Scott's "blonde heroines" and "dark heroines," but Austen's heroines cannot be classified. Can any reader imagine Elizabeth Bennet or Emma Woodhouse waiting seven years for a Wentworth? Or Wentworth falling in love with a Fanny Price?

The Austen heroine possesses a genuine, although limited freedom – limited by situation and guided by principle. As the example of Henry Crawford demonstrates, "freedom" that is not so guided is useless – even to Crawford himself – and illusory. It can be dangerous as well, as Crawford's behavior toward women demonstrates. Every Austen heroine has sufficient leeway to think, decide, and by doing so eventually achieve her desires. First, as Emma learns, she must know what her desires are. Until she does, Emma's apparently total "freedom" – as mistress of her own household, subordinate to no one – is nearly as self-defeating as the Crawfords', and likewise potentially harmful to others. The apparent freedom of Mary Crawford – young, intelligent, and independently wealthy – is illusory, limited not only by the social restrictions imposed on unmarried women, whatever their social position, but by her unquestioning submission to the standards of fashionable London.

The novels in fact are on the side of freedom and of feeling – although with inevitable limits, determined first by morality, secondarily by social convention and status. All societies impose limits on their members, a necessity Austen acknowledges. Consequently, her novels can probably never be acceptable to extreme romantics or to political and social radicals. Nevertheless, Emerson's judgment that the way of life she portrays is miserably "cramped and narrow" (Emerson, 1:28) can be contradicted by a careful reading and subjectively refuted by the sense of exhilaration that *Pride and Prejudice*, for example, can produce. The heroines know what they "ought" to expect, but they demand more, and get it. The freedom they exercise is limited of course, but it is meaningful only because it has limits. The seeming possibility of unlimited choice is likely to prove bewildering and frustrating, and must prove illusory in any case. The social world of the novels may seem narrow to modern readers, its manners and morals often rigid and restrictive, but it is a world on a human scale, and knowing the limits, the heroines can go beyond them on occasion.

Notes

Chapter One

1. *Minor Works*, vol. 6 of *The Works of Jane Austen*, ed. R. W. Chapman (London: Oxford University Press, 1965); hereafter cited in text as *Minor Works*.

2. *Jane Austen's Letters*, 2d ed., ed. R. W. Chapman (London: Oxford University Press, 1952), 2; hereafter cited in text as *Letters*.

3. Quoted in James E. Austen-Leigh, *A Memoir of Jane Austen*, ed. R. W. Chapman (London: Oxford University Press, 1926); hereafter cited in text as *Memoir*.

Chapter Two

1. Virginia Woolf, "Jane Austen," in Literary Essays (London: Hogarth Press, 1966), 1:146.

2. *Northanger Abbey* and *Persuasion*, ed. R. W. Chapman (London: Oxford University Press, 1965); all passages from *Northanger Abbey* quoted in the text are from this edition.

3. Austen divided her novels into what she called "volumes" rather than parts. Her terminology is used throughout this study.

4. Allison Sulloway, *Jane Austen and the Province of Womanhood* (Philadelphia: University of Pennsylvania Press, 1989), 55.

Chapter Three

1. *Sense and Sensibility*, ed. R. W. Chapman (London: Oxford University Press, 1965); all passages quoted in the text are from this edition.

Chapter Four

1. *Pride and Prejudice*, ed. R. W. Chapman (London: Oxford University Press, 1965); all passages quoted in the text are from this edition.

2. Rachel Brownstein, "Jane Austen: Irony and Authority," *Women's Studies* 15 (1988): 64.

3. Marilyn Butler, *Jane Austen and the War of Ideas* (London: Oxford University Press, 1975), 82; hereafter cited in text.

Chapter Five

1. Quotations from readers contemporary to Jane Austen are from "Opinions of *Mansfield Park* and *Emma*," pp. 431-40, in *Minor Works*.

2. Reginald Farrer, "Jane Austen," *Quarterly Review*, July 1917; reprinted in and quoted here from *Jane Austen: The Critical Heritage*, ed. B. C. Southam (London: Routledge & Kegan Paul, 1968, 1987), 2:264; hereafter cited in text.

3. C. S. Lewis, "A Note on Jane Austen," *Essays in Criticism* 4 (October 1954); reprinted in and quoted here from *Jane Austen: A Collection of Critical Essays*, ed. Ian Watt (Englewood Cliffs, N.J.: Prentice-Hall, 1963), 31.

4. *Mansfield Park*, ed. R. W. Chapman (London: Oxford University Press, 1965); all passages quoted in the text are from this edition.

5. Lionel Trilling, "Mansfield Park," in *The Opposing Self* (New York: Viking Press, 1955); reprinted in and quoted here from *Jane Austen: The Critical Heritage*, ed. Southam, 2:137; hereafter cited in text.

6. Edmund Wilson, "A Long Talk about Jane Austen," in *Classics and Commercials* (New York: 1950); reprinted in and quoted here from *Jane Austen: A Collection of Critical Essays*, ed. Watt.

Chapter Six

1. Marvin Mudrick, *Jane Austen: Irony as Defense and Discovery* (Princeton, N.J.: Princeton University Press, 1952), 202-3; hereafter cited in text.

2. *Emma*, ed. R. W. Chapman (London: Oxford University Press, 1965); all passages quoted in the text are from this edition.

3. Julia Prewitt Brown, *Jane Austen's Novels: Social Change and Literary Form* (Cambridge, Mass.: Harvard University Press, 1979); hereafter cited in text.

4. Alistair Duckworth, *The Improvement of the Estate: A Study of Jane Austen's Novels* (Baltimore: Johns Hopkins University Press, 1971), 216.

5. A. C. Bradley, untitled lecture.

6. Q. D. Leavis, "A Critical Theory of Jane Austen's Writings," *Scrutiny* 10 (June 1941): 83.

Chapter Seven

1. *Northanger Abbey* and *Persuasion*, ed. R. W. Chapman (London: Oxford University Press, 1965); all passages from *Persuasion* quoted in the text are from this edition.

2. See the appendix to *The Novels of Jane Austen*, vol. 5 (*Northanger Abbey* and *Persuasion*) of *The Works of Jane Austen*, ed. R. W. Chapman (London: Oxford University Press, 1965).

Chapter Eight

1. All passages from "The Watsons" quoted in the text are from *Minor Works*.

2. See *Minor Works*.

3. All passages from "Sanditon" quoted in the text are from *Minor Works*.

4. Mary Lascelles, *Jane Austen and Her Art* (London: Oxford University Press, 1939), 39; hereafter cited in text.

5. See, for example, *Sanditon*, published under the byline "By Jane Austen and Another Lady" [Anne Telscombe] (Boston: Houghton Mifflin, 1975).

Chapter Nine

1. Unsigned notice, *British Critic*, February 1813; reprinted in and quoted here from *Jane Austen: The Critical Heritage*, ed. Southam, 1:40.

2. Unsigned notice, *British Critic*, July 1816; reprinted in and quoted here from *Jane Austen: The Critical Heritage*, ed. Southam, 1:71.

3. Unsigned notice, *British Critic*, March 1813; reprinted in and quoted here from *Jane Austen: The Critical Heritage*, ed. Southam, 1:46.

4. Walter Scott, an unsigned review of *Emma*, *Quarterly Review*, October 1815; reprinted in and quoted here from *Jane Austen: The Critical Heritage*, ed. Southam, 1:67; hereafter cited in text as Scott 1815.

5. Unsigned review of *The Life and Adventures of Peter Wilkins*, *Retrospective Review*, 1823 [no month]; reprinted in and quoted here from *Jane Austen: The Critical Heritage*, ed. Southam, 1:106.

6. Quoted on p. 5 of *The Novels of Jane Austen*, vol. 5 of *The Works of Jane Austen*; hereafter cited in text as *Novels*.

7. R. W. Whateley, review of Northanger Abbey and Persuasion, *Quarterly Review*, January 1821; reprinted in and quoted here from *Jane Austen: The Critical Heritage*, ed. Southam, 1:95; hereafter cited in text.

8. George Henry Lewes, "The Novels of Jane Austen," *Blackwood's Edinburgh Magazine*, July 1869, 99-113; reprinted in and quoted here from *Jane Austen: The Critical Heritage*, ed. Southam, 1:157; hereafter cited in text.

9. Extracts from letters, *The Brontës: Their Friendships, Lives, and Correspondence*, ed. T. J. Wise and J. A. Symington; reprinted in and quoted here from *Jane Austen: The Critical Heritage*, ed. Southam, 1:126.

10. Letter of 5 November 1855 from Elizabeth Barret Browning to Ruskin, *Letters of Elizabeth Barret Browning*, ed. F. G. Kenyon (1897); reprinted in and quoted here from *Jane Austen: The Critical Heritage*, ed. Southam, 1:25.

11. *Journals of Ralph Waldo Emerson,* ed. E. W. Emerson (1913); reprinted in and quoted here from *Jane Austen: The Critical Heritage,* ed. Southam, 1:28; hereafter cited in text.

12. Unsigned obituary for Anthony Trollope, *Times* (London), 7 December 1882; reprinted in and quoted here from *Jane Austen: The Critical Heritage,* ed. Southam, 2:175.

13. Richard Simpson, review of *Memoir, North British Review,* April 1870; reprinted in and quoted here from *Jane Austen: The Critical Heritage,* ed. Southam, 1:243; hereafter cited in text.

14. Letter of 23 June 1883 from Henry James to "Pellew," 23; reprinted in and quoted here from *Jane Austen: The Critical Heritage,* ed. Southam, 2:179.

15. Henry James, "The Lesson of Balzac" (1905); reprinted in and quoted here from *Jane Austen: The Critical Heritage,* ed. Southam, 2:230.

16. Henry James, "The New Novel" (1914); reprinted in and quoted here from *Jane Austen: The Critical Heritage,* ed. Southam, 2:231.

17. Virginia Woolf, quoted in *Jane Austen: The Critical Heritage,* ed. Southam, 2:283.

18. D. W. Harding, "Regulated Hatred: An Aspect of the Work of Jane Austen," *Scrutiny* 8 (1939): 346-62; reprinted in and quoted here from *Jane Austen: A Collection of Critical Essays,* ed. Watt, 170; hereafter cited in text.

19. Reuben Brower, "Light, Bright, and Sparkling: Irony and Fiction in Pride and Prejudice," reprinted in and quoted here from *Jane Austen: A Collection of Critical Essays,* ed. Watt, 62; hereafter cited in text.

Chapter Ten

1. Letter of 1913 from Joseph Conrad to H. G. Wells, quoted in *Jane Austen: The Critical Heritage,* ed. Southam, 2:300.

2. Lionel Stevenson, *The English Novel: A Panorama* (Boston: Houghton Mifflin, 1960), 181.

3. Henri Bergson, "Laughter," in *Comedy,* ed. Wylie Sypher (New York: Doubleday and Co., 1958), 64.

4. Graham Hough, "Narrative and Dialogue in Jane Austen," *Critical Quarterly,* Autumn 1970, 209; hereafter cited in text.

Selected Bibliography

PRIMARY WORKS

Novels

Sense and Sensibility. London: T. Egerton, 1811.
Pride and Prejudice. London: T. Egerton, 1813.
Mansfield Park. London: T. Egerton, 1814.
Emma. London: John Murray, 1816.
Northanger Abbey and *Persuasion.* London: John Murray, 1818.
The Novels of Jane Austen. 5 vols. 3d ed. Edited by R. W. Chapman. London: Oxford University Press, 1933. The standard edition of the novels.

Miscellaneous Writings

Minor Works. Vol. 6 of *The Works of Jane Austen,* edited by R. W. Chapman. London: Oxford University Press, 1965.

Letters

Jane Austen's Letters. 2d ed. Edited by R. W. Chapman. London: Oxford University Press, 1952.

SECONDARY WORKS

Austen-Leigh, J. E. *A Memoir of Jane Austen.* Edited by R. W. Chapman. London: Oxford University Press, 1926. Presents Austen as a model of piety and Victorian gentility.

Brown, Julia Prewitt. *Jane Austen's Novels: Social Change and Literary Form.* Cambridge, Mass.: Harvard University Press, 1979. A sensitive blending of feminist concerns with more traditional criticism. Describes Austen's novels as being concerned with both the development of feminine consciousness and "the actual and immediate quality of social existence."

Butler, Marilyn. *Jane Austen and the War of Ideas.* London: Oxford University Press, 1975. A thorough study of the ideological implications of Austen's work, containing significant criticism as well.

Duckworth, Alistair. *The Improvement of the Estate: A Study of Jane Austen's Novels.* Baltimore: Johns Hopkins University Press, 1971. A pioneering study, relating Austen's fiction to contemporary social issues and seeing the novels as essentially conservative in their implications.

Harris, Jocelyn. *Jane Austen's Art of Memory.* Cambridge: Cambridge University Press, 1989. A thorough study of Austen's use of literary sources, including William Shakespeare, Samuel Richardson, Samuel Johnson, Alexander Pope, and John Milton.

Hodge, Janet Aiken. *Only a Novel: The Double Life of Jane Austen.* New York: Coward McCann, 1972. Perceptive, sympathetic, yet unsentimental popular biography.

Hough, Graham. "Narrative and Dialogue in Jane Austen." *Critical Quarterly* 12 (Autumn 1970): 201-29. An essential study, examining the nature of Austen's "realism" and the ideological significance of the novels, as well as offering a penetrating examination of style and narrative technique.

Johnson, Claudia. *Jane Austen: Women, Politics, and the Novel.* Chicago: University of Chicago Press, 1988. Demonstrates the relationship of Austen's fiction to "a largely feminine tradition of political novels."

Lascelles, Mary. *Jane Austen and Her Art.* London: Oxford University Press, 1939. A basic work, offering a perceptive examination of Austen's technique, in the widest possible sense of the term.

Morgan, Susan. *In the Meantime: Character and Perception in Jane Austen's Fiction.* Chicago: University of Chicago Press, 1980. A sympathetic study, seeing Austen's presentation of "ordinary life, the romance to be found in ordinary circumstances" as basic to her work.

Mudrick, Marvin. *Jane Austen: Irony as Defense and Discovery.* Princeton, N.J.: Princeton University Press, 1952. Penetrating criticism, combined with a good deal of forced reading, all intended to reveal a sharply satirical Austen, rebelling against the moral and social conventions of her day.

Page, Norman. *The Language of Jane Austen.* New York: Barnes and Noble, 1972. An informative but nontechnical analysis.

Poovey, Mary. *The Proper Lady and the Woman Writer: Ideology as Style in the Works of Mary Wollstonecraft, Mary Shelly, and Jane Austen.* Chicago: University of Chicago Press, 1984. Essentially an ideological study, placing Austen in relation to a continuing feminist tradition.

Southam, B. C. *Jane Austen's Literary Manuscripts: A Study of the Novelist's Development through the Surviving Papers.* Oxford University Press, 1964. Includes the juvenilia, "Lady Susan," "The Watsons," "Sanditon," and the reconciliation scenes in *Persuasion.*

———, ed. *Jane Austen: The Critical Heritage.* 2 vols. London: Routledge and Kegan Paul, 1968, 1987. Both an anthology and a history of Austen criticism, a basic source for the period covered, 1811-1938.

____, ed. *Critical Essays on Jane Austen*. London: Routledge and Kegan Paul, 1968. A valuable collection of essential modern criticism.

Sulloway, Allison. *Jane Austen and the Province of Womanhood*. Philadelphia: University of Pennsylvania Press, 1989. Sees Austen as a "protofeminist," satirically assailing "destructive myths and assumptions" concerning women.

Watt, Ian, ed. *Jane Austen: A Collection of Critical Essays*. Englewood Cliffs, N.J.: Prentice-Hall, 1963. An essential collection of Austen criticism from the early 1920s to the early 1960s, with a valuable introductory survey of Austen scholarship and criticism by the editor.

Weinsheimer, Joel, ed. *Jane Austen Today*. Athens, Ga.: University of Georgia Press, 1975. Valuable collection of general essays, supplementing Watt's collection. Donald Greene's "The Myth of Limitation" is particularly notable.

Index

The Author

John Lauber holds a doctorate in English from the University of Washington. He taught at the universities of New Mexico and Idaho before moving to the University of Alberta, Canada, at which he spent the greater part of his career. Professor Lauber has always been deeply interested in the prose and poetry of early nineteenth-century England and has been a lifelong reader and admirer of Jane Austen's novels, in particular. He is the author of *Sir Walter Scott* in Twayne's English Authors Series and of two essays on Byron. He has also published a number of papers in the areas of Canadian and American literature as well as a two-volume biography of Mark Twain, *The Making of Mark Twain* and *The Inventions of Mark Twain*. Now retired, he lives in Victoria, British Columbia, Canada.